The Healthy 5-Ingredient
AIR FRYER
Cookbook

The Healthy 5-Ingredient
AIR FRYER
Cookbook

70
EASY RECIPES TO
BAKE, FRY, OR ROAST YOUR
FAVORITE FOODS

BONNIE MATTHEWS AND DAWN E. HALL
Photos by Bonnie Matthews

Skyhorse Publishing

Skyhorse Publishing books may be purchased in bulk at special discounts for sales promotion, corporate gifts, fund-raising, or educational purposes. Special editions can also be created to specifications. For details, contact the Special Sales Department, Skyhorse Publishing, 307 West 36th Street, 11th Floor, New York, NY 10018 or info@skyhorsepublishing.com.

Skyhorse® and Skyhorse Publishing® are registered trademarks of Skyhorse Publishing, Inc.®, a Delaware corporation.

Visit our website at www.skyhorsepublishing.com.

10 9 8 7 6

Library of Congress Cataloging-in-Publication Data is available on file.

Cover design by Abigail Gehring
Cover image by Bonnie Matthews

Print ISBN: 978-1-5107-4159-1
Ebook ISBN: 978-1-5107-4160-7

Printed in China

This book is dedicated to the memory of my Dad and my brother Larry, who shared my passion for cooking and photography. —BM

This book is dedicated to my Mom, Donnetha, who is the reason why I love to cook. She just so happens to be the best teacher, culinary or otherwise, I've ever had. —DH

Contents

Acknowledgments ix

Introduction xi

CHAPTER 1
Breakfast: Start Your Busy Week Off Right 1

Florentine Breakfast Casserole 3
Blueberry French Toast Muffins 4
The "Hard-Boiled" Air Fry Egg 6
Traditional Deviled Eggs 7
Avocado Deviled Eggs 7
Veggie Frittata 8
Sweet Potato Toasts 11

CHAPTER 2
Lunch and Dinner: Mouthwatering Meat and Veggie Mains 13

Portabella Fajitas 15
Teriyaki Chicken with Broccoli and Carrots 16
Salmon with Kale and Mushrooms in Truffle Oil 18
Baja Pork Fajitas 21
Vegetable Spring Rolls 22
Flatbread Veggie Pizzas 25
Herb-Crusted Pork Chops 26
Simple Salmon with Pea Puree 29
Crusted Pork Medallions with Rubbed Sage 30
Sriracha Shrimp 33

Jerk Tempeh with Toasted Coconut Cauli Rice 34
Black Bean and Sweet Potato Burgers 37
Falafel Kebabs 38
Turkey Koftas 41
Summer Veggie Kebabs 42
Pistachio-Crusted Shrimp with Asian Dipping Sauce 44
"N'awlins" Tofu 47
Moroccan Chicken Skewers 48
Zesty Orange Rib-Eye Skewers 51
Shish Kebabs 52

CHAPTER 3
Sides (with Some Extra Love for the Sweet Potato) 55

Stuffed Cremini Mushrooms 57
Easy Balsamic-Roasted Vegetables 58
Farro with Shaved Brussels Sprouts 61
Roasted Stuffed Tomatoes 62
Buffalo Brussels Sprouts 65
Eggplant Bruschetta with Roasted Polenta 66
Lemon-Pepper Green Beans 69
Asian Sweet Potato and Shrimp Crisps 70
Crispy Cajun Sweet Potato Wedges 73
Sweet Potato Hash 74
Curried Sweet Potato Fritters 77
Ancho Sweet Potato Strings 78

CHAPTER 4

Snacks and Chips: No-Guilt
Munchies for Any Time of Day   81

Garlic-Parmesan Chickpeas   83
Roasted Garlic and Bean Dip   84
Roasted Beet Hummus   87
Everything Pita Chips   88
Sweet and Spicy Almonds   91
Parsnip Chips with Garam Masala   92
Spiced Apple Chips   95
Polenta Fries   96
Chipotle Rutabaga Chips   99
Chili-Lime Taro Chips   100
Air-Fried Plantains with Avocado-Mango
    Relish   103
Montego Bay Turnip Chips   104

CHAPTER 5

Kid-Friendly Foods: Tempting Treats
for Even the Pickiest of Eaters   107

Vegan Taquitos   109
Italian Quesadillas   110
Zucchini Soldiers   113
Granola Wedges   114
Mini Corn Pups   117
Veggie and Chickpea Nuggets   118
BBQ Tempeh Sticks   121
Grilled Cheese and Grilled PBB Sandwiches   122
Broccoli Tots   125

CHAPTER 6

The Sweet Spot: Guilt-Free Desserts
to Satisfy Your Sweet Tooth   127

Banana-Coconut Rolls   129
Blackberry Cheesecake Chimichangas   130
Pear-Kumquat Tart   133
Best-Ever 5-Ingredient Air Fryer Chocolate
    Cake   134
Strawberry Crisp   137
Apple Galette   138
Gingered Almond Cookies   141

Conversion Charts   143
Index   145
About the Authors and Photographer   151

Acknowledgments

I'd like to thank Alysia Gadson, my friend and neighbor, who tasted all the recipes and provided great feedback in helping create this book. —BM

I'd like to thank my entire family for their support with all that I do and my friend, Bonnie Matthews, for stopping by The Hood Kitchen, allowing us to meet and start this awesome partnership.—DH

Introduction

What the heck is an air fryer anyway?

Glad you asked! The air fryer is a unique countertop electric machine that uses circulated hot air to bake and grill foods. It's nothing like an electric deep fat fryer that you fill with cooking oil. Instead, the air fryer requires no deep vat of oil at all; just spray light amounts of cooking spray on foods and insert them into the machine. Because you use very little or no cooking oil, you can create healthier meals without all that extra fat.

The air fryer browns and crisps most foods, just like your oven, but it's very easy to clean up with a simple removable basket that washes up fast. Its self-contained quiet fan and heat element warm up very quickly and, unlike your oven, it does not heat up your entire kitchen. (It also traps a lot of the food odors while cooking, which is a bonus!)

The fryer typically comes with 3 main parts that are all easy to clean and simple to handle. The main countertop electric air fryer comes with a pan that is inserted into the appliance. Within that pan is a basket with a handle that holds the food items. The basket base has holes in it to allow for any extra oil, or fats from the food, to drip down so the food isn't sitting in unnecessary extra fats.

Who Would Benefit from the Air Fryer?

We think the air fryer is great for singles, couples, college kids, and small families. Heck, even trailer or cabin campers who have access to electricity would enjoy using it. Most models are very light, and each offers a quick and easy way to make simple meals and snacks. We think you'll be surprised at how fun it is to cook with!

What Kind Should You Get?

We discovered a wide range of price points and brands to choose from. They come with various features, options, and accessories (which can be purchased separately).

We created the recipes in this book using air fryer cooking methods, but we've also created some fun recipes utilizing the accessories, such as:

Shallow Baking Pan

This baking tin is great for frittatas, pizzas, or for cooking an item where you wish to retain the juices or sauce.

Cake Barrel

Complete with handle, this baking tin works great for cakes, breads, breakfast casseroles, or any meal that might require a deeper pot, such as chili or stew, where you want to retain the liquid.

Metal Rack and Multi-Purpose Skewer Rack

The metal grill layer has more than a few good uses! You can place it over a lighter food item, such as a tortilla, to help keep the food in place while cooking. The double grill layer comes with skewers that allow you to cook kebabs, and you can cook the skewered food on top while cooking other foods underneath.

Mini Silicone Cupcake Pan

This is great for egg cups, healthier baked sweet treats where you want to control your portion size, and any little baked anythings, really!

Even if you don't purchase the extra accessories, you can use oven-safe cookware in the machine, such as ceramic ramekins, silicone single muffin cups, and small metal baking pans.

A Note on the Recipes

Because there are so many brands of machines, we've found a lot of variables with cooking times and temps. For this reason, we provide a cook temperature, a range for cooking times, and visual indicators of doneness for all our recipes. There may be some differences with your specific machine.

Because we're all strapped for time, we wanted to create simple meals that can be made with very few ingredients—5, in fact. The 5 ingredients in each recipe are things you may or may not have on hand. Many of the recipes also call for additional "pantry items" that are staples in most kitchen (see page xiv). We also call for a lot of prechopped veggies or premade sauces to save on time. Always check the labels to be sure you're buying the cleanest products with ingredients you can pronounce.

Why We Wrote This Book

With people becoming more health conscious and seeking fresh new ways to introduce nutritious foods into their diets, it's no wonder the air fryer has become so popular. Folks are watching their waistlines, their cashflow, and their clocks. A lot more people are choosing to prepare food at home so they can eat cleaner and know what's in it.

This book is a fun exploration of our collaboration in the kitchen. Though we are both self-taught cooks with different cooking styles, we each seek healthier foods that don't compromise on flavor. We've incorporated an abundance of world flavors with influences from all over. And with plant-based foods gaining more popularity, we've included many vegetarian and vegan options throughout.

With the air fryer as your kitchen's backbone, you too, can discover fresh and easy ways to elevate your meals, whether you're new to cooking or just new to air fryers. With this book, we'll help you maintain a conscious effort for making better food choices.

Your Air Fryer Pantry

We are all about saving time and not fretting over what to buy or prepare for meals! Having some of these items handy will not only help you make the meals in this book but will also help destress your shopping experience.

Spice Staples

Chili powder

Garlic powder (not garlic salt)

Ground cinnamon

Italian seasoning

Onion powder

Paprika: sweet (but smoked can "spice up" a recipe)

Pepper: freshly ground black and cayenne

Rubbed sage

Salt: kosher and Himalayan pink

Other Staples

Oil: vegetable, olive, and coconut (optional)

Cooking spray (or spritzer for oil)

Breadcrumbs: regular and panko, plain and seasoned

Eggs

Fresh garlic

Fresh citrus: lemons and limes

Out of breadcrumbs? Make your own:

Preheat the air fryer to 300°F for 5 minutes. Place 1 slice of your favorite bread in the fry basket (use an insert if more crumbs are needed). Cook for 7–10 minutes per side. Remove and cool completely. Pulse in a food processor until fine crumbs form. Store in an airtight container for up to 5 days.

Baking staples

Almond meal/flour

Baking soda

Baking powder

Coconut flour

Honey (raw) or agave nectar

Sugar: coconut and brown

Vanilla extract (pure, not imitation)

Whole wheat flour

Equipment

Vegetable slicer or mandolin

Meat or kitchen thermometer

Cookie sheet

Parchment paper

Aluminum foil

Mixing bowls of various sizes

Air fryer accessories that fit your machine

CHAPTER 1
Breakfast: Start Your Busy Week Off Right

Florentine Breakfast Casserole

This is a great recipe for getting the kids involved. Let them add their favorite veggies or breakfast meats, and they'll be happy to eat a meal they helped prepare. Serve with fresh fruit on the side.

MAKES 4 WEDGES

Ingredients:

1½ cups frozen tater tots or hash browns

¼ cup firmly packed chopped fresh spinach

2 large eggs

2 tablespoons milk

2 tablespoons grated Parmesan cheese

Pantry items:

Cake barrel

Cooking spray

Kosher salt

Freshly ground black pepper

Aluminum foil

Directions:

Preheat the air fryer to 400°F for 5 minutes. Lightly coat the cake barrel with cooking spray.

Cook the tater tots in the fry basket for 7–10 minutes. Crumble the tots into the bottom of the cake barrel and top with the chopped spinach.

In a small bowl, scramble the eggs and milk and season with a pinch of salt and pepper. Pour over the potato and spinach mixture and cover with aluminum foil.

Cook until the eggs are set, 20–25 minutes. Remove the foil and sprinkle the cheese on top. Cook, uncovered, until lightly browned on top, 3–5 minutes more.

Blueberry French Toast Muffins

There's no need to shy away from all carbs. We love Ezekiel 4:9 Sprouted Whole Grain Bread in this recipe because of its firm texture. Look for it in the freezer case of the natural foods section in your supermarket. Coconut sugar is a slightly healthier, more natural sugar made from the nectar of coconut flowers. Look for it in the natural foods section, but if you can't find it, you can substitute brown sugar.

MAKES 7 MUFFINS

Ingredients:

2 large eggs

¼ cup + 2 tablespoons milk

1 tablespoon coconut sugar

4 to 6 slices stale, sprouted whole-grain bread, cubed

½ cup fresh blueberries

Pantry items:

Mini silicone cupcake pan

Directions:

In a small bowl, whisk together the eggs, milk, and sugar. Gently fold in the bread and blueberries. Cover and refrigerate for at least 2 hours.

Preheat the air fryer to 320°F for 5 minutes.

Place the cupcake pan in the fry basket. Spoon the muffin batter evenly into each cup. Cook until a toothpick inserted into the center of one comes out clean, 20–25 minutes.

The "Hard-Boiled" Air Fry Egg

Hard-boiled eggs are a great protein-rich grab-and-go breakfast item. Enjoy one with a little salt and pepper or try it sliced on top of Sweet Potato Toasts (page 11).

MAKES 4 HARD-BOILED EGGS

Ingredients:

4 large eggs

Pantry items:

Metal rack

Ice

Water

Directions:

Place the metal rack into the fry basket and preheat the fryer to 250°F for 5 minutes.

Place the eggs on the rack. Set a timer for 20 minutes. Allow the eggs to sit for an additional minute while you prepare an ice bath (2–3 cups ice in 1–1½ cups water).

Place the cooked eggs into the ice bath and cool completely. Refrigerate for grab-and-go breakfasts or turn into deviled eggs (below).

Traditional Deviled Eggs

MAKES 8 DEVILED EGGS

Ingredients:
4 "Hard-Boiled" Air Fry Eggs (above)

2–3 tablespoons mayonnaise

1 tablespoon relish (optional)

½ teaspoon prepared mustard

Paprika (optional)

Pantry items:
Kosher salt

Freshly ground black pepper

Directions:
Peel the eggs and cut them in half lengthwise. Scoop the yolks into a bowl and mash with a fork. Add the mayonnaise, relish (if using), mustard, and a pinch of salt and pepper. Mix well until smooth. Spoon the mixture into the egg whites and sprinkle with the paprika, if using.

Avocado Deviled Eggs

MAKES 8 DEVILED EGGS

Ingredients:
4 "Hard-Boiled" Air Fry Eggs (above)

½ avocado

1–2 tablespoons mayonnaise

4 cherry tomatoes, halved (optional)

Chopped cilantro (optional)

Pantry items:
Kosher salt

Freshly ground black pepper

Directions:
Peel the eggs and cut them in half lengthwise. Scoop the yolks into a bowl and mash with a fork. Add the avocado, mayonnaise, and a pinch of salt and pepper. Mix well until smooth. Spoon the mixture into the egg whites and garnish with the cherry tomatoes or cilantro, if desired.

Veggie Frittata

You can make this frittata with whatever vegetables you have on hand, including any leftover Sweet Potato Hash (page 74). Some people believe Himalayan pink salt is healthier and cleaner than other types of salt. You can generally find it with the other spices at your grocery store; if not, try the natural foods section. Substitute kosher salt, if desired.

MAKES 2 SERVINGS

Ingredients:

3 large eggs, whisked

1 cup fresh spinach, coarsely chopped

4 or 5 cremini mushrooms, thinly sliced

3–5 oil-packed sun-dried tomatoes, chopped (or use those from the salad bar!)

2 tablespoons grated Gruyère cheese

Pantry items:

Shallow baking dish

Cooking spray

Italian seasoning

Himalayan pink salt

Freshly ground black pepper

Aluminum foil

Directions:

Preheat the air fryer to 320°F for 5 minutes. Spray the baking pan with cooking spray.

In a medium bowl, mix together the eggs, spinach, mushrooms, sun-dried tomatoes, and cheese. Add a pinch of Italian seasoning, salt, and pepper. Pour into the pan, and cover with aluminum foil.

Place the pan in the fry basket and cook 8–9 minutes. Remove the foil and cook until the eggs are set, 7–8 minutes more. Cut into quarters or halves and serve.

Sweet Potato Toasts

Use these taters to elevate your morning toast routine: top them with avocado, sliced tomato, "hard-boiled" eggs (page 6), or almond butter and sliced bananas.

MAKES 4 SLICES

Ingredients:
1 medium sweet potato, skin on, cut lengthwise into ½-inch-thick slices
1 tablespoon olive oil

Pantry items:
Himalayan pink salt

Directions:
Preheat the air fryer to 360°F for 5 minutes.

Place the potato in a microwave-safe bowl, cover with a paper towel, and cook on high until tender, 2 minutes.

Lightly coat each side of the toasts with the oil and sprinkle with a pinch of salt. Cook in the fry basket for 5 minutes. Flip the toasts and cook until browned and the edges begin to crisp, about 5 minutes more.

CHAPTER 2
Lunch and Dinner: Mouthwatering Meat and Veggie Mains

Portabella Fajitas

If you forgot it was Meatless Monday, try this plant-based recipe for Taco Tuesday! Serve the fajitas with warmed whole wheat tortillas and any combo of accoutrement—salsa, avocado, or cheese. Look in your supermarket's produce section for the fajita veggies, typically sliced and packaged in-house.

MAKES 4 FAJITAS

Ingredients:

2 tablespoons olive oil

2 teaspoons fajita or taco seasoning

1 package (9–12 ounces) fresh presliced fajita vegetables (mixed-colored peppers and onion)

1 portabella mushroom cap, stem and gills removed, sliced into ½-inch-thick strips

Pantry items:

Cake barrel

Directions:

Preheat the air fryer to 360°F for 5 minutes.

In a medium bowl, combine the olive oil and seasoning. Add the vegetables and toss until all the veggies are coated in the spice mixture. Add the portabella slices and gently toss.

Transfer the vegetables to the cake barrel and set in the fryer. Cook until the veggies are tender, 8–10 minutes.

Teriyaki Chicken with Broccoli and Carrots

Whether you're bulking up or shredding at the gym, this meal is low carb and loaded with protein. It's also great for meal prep. Portion out the teriyaki sauce and ½ cup cooked brown rice for a meal you can take with you.

MAKES 2 SERVINGS

Ingredients:

For the chicken:
2 boneless, skinless chicken breasts (4 ounces each)
1½ cups broccoli florets
1½ cups coarsely chopped carrots

For the teriyaki sauce:
2 tablespoons cornstarch
½ cup Bragg Liquid Aminos or low-sodium soy sauce
3 tablespoons coconut sugar

Pantry items:

Kosher salt
Freshly ground black pepper
Garlic powder
Parchment paper
Metal rack

Directions:

For the chicken: Preheat the air fryer to 360°F for 5 minutes.

Season the chicken breasts, broccoli, and carrots with a pinch of salt, pepper, and garlic powder.

Place a chicken breast squarely on a piece of parchment paper and top with half of the vegetables (you can also cook each separately). Evenly gather two sides of the paper and fold them until they lie down on the vegetables. Fold the ends up to seal the pouch. Repeat with the remaining chicken and vegetables.

Place the pouches in the fry basket and place the metal rack on top to keep the paper from opening. Cook until the chicken's internal temperature has reached 165°F, 20–25 minutes.

For the teriyaki sauce: Place the cornstarch in a small bowl and add a little bit of the liquid aminos, stirring until completely smooth. Whisk together the remaining liquid aminos and coconut sugar in a small saucepan. Bring to a boil over medium-high heat, whisking constantly, until the sugar is dissolved. Whisk in the cornstarch mixture and boil, whisking, until the sauce thickens and is very smooth, 1 minute. Cool briefly before drizzling over the chicken and veggies.

Salmon with Kale and Mushrooms in Truffle Oil

It's widely known that salmon is a good source of protein and healthy fats, but did you know that it matters how that fish was raised? Though there are reputable, sustainable, and responsibly farmed fisheries around the world, the labeling for these products is often unclear. If your pocketbook can afford it, wild-caught Pacific salmon is the better way to go. Learn your species—if it's Atlantic salmon, it's been farmed.

You may wish to make the kale and mushrooms first and keep them warm while you prepare the fish. Lacinato kale is also called dinosaur kale. Its leaves are longer, smoother, and less frilly than standard curly kale—and more tender.

MAKES 2 SERVINGS

Ingredients:

For the salmon:

2 fillets (3–4 ounces each) wild-caught salmon, with or without skin
½ teaspoon garlic powder
¼ teaspoon paprika
2 lemon wedges

For the kale and mushrooms:

1 bunch lacinato kale
6 medium cremini mushrooms, thinly sliced
1 teaspoon white truffle oil
1½ teaspoons grated or shaved Parmesan cheese

Pantry items:

Olive oil
Himalayan pink salt
Freshly ground black pepper
Cooking spray
Cake barrel
Metal rack

Directions:

For the salmon: Allow the fish to come to room temperature, about 20 minutes.
Preheat the air fryer to 400°F for 5 minutes.

Set the fish, skin-side down, on a clean surface. Rub with olive oil and coat with the garlic powder, paprika, and a pinch of salt and pepper.

Spray the bottom of the fry basket with cooking spray and carefully set in the 2 fillets, skin-side down. Cook until flaky and opaque, 6–7 minutes.

For the kale and mushrooms: Preheat the air fryer to 360°F for 5 minutes.

Rinse and pat dry the kale leaves. With a sharp knife, cut along the hard center stem on either side and cut out the stem. Take the remaining leaf and cut crosswise into 2-inch strips (they will wilt when cooked). Place the kale strips in a medium bowl and spray with a little cooking spray. Massage the kale lightly for about 15 seconds to bruise it and make it more tender.

Toss the kale and mushrooms in the cake barrel and spray with a little cooking spray. Add a generous pinch of salt and pepper. Set the metal rack on top to prevent the kale from flying up into the heating element.

Cook for 6 minutes. Open the air fryer, stir, replace the insert, and cook until desired tenderness, about 2 minutes more. When done, drizzle with the white truffle oil and sprinkle with the cheese. Serve with the salmon and a lemon wedge.

Note: Some air fryers will produce different results. If you find your kale is drying out too much, add 1 teaspoon water, cover the cake barrel with aluminum foil and the metal rack, and cook until tender.

Baja Pork Fajitas

There are a few really good brands of prepared sauces on the market that are all natural and don't contain high fructose corn syrup or added fillers. And they make your meal time prep super easy! We love the Frontera brand with its clean ingredients and fantastically authentic taste. Serve the fajitas with warmed whole wheat tortillas, chopped cilantro, lime wedges, and a few crumbles of cotija cheese.

MAKES 4 FAJITAS

Ingredients:

2 boneless country-style pork ribs (or about 1½ cups diced lean pork of any kind)

¾ cup diced bell pepper (save yourself time and buy a colorful medley from the produce aisle)

½ cup Frontera Garlicky Carnitas Slow Cook Sauce with Lime + Chipotle (see Note)

3 cloves garlic, minced

½ can (14.5 ounces) fire-roasted diced tomatoes with green chilies and garlic (or slightly more, if desired)

Pantry items:

Cake barrel

Cooking spray

Directions:

Preheat the air fryer to 390°F for 5 minutes. Spray the cake barrel with a little cooking spray.

In a medium bowl, mix together the pork, peppers, sauce, and garlic. Transfer the mixture to the cake barrel.

Cook for 4 minutes. Stir and cook another 2 minutes. Stir in the tomatoes and cook until the vegetables are tender and the pork reaches 145°F, 6–8 minutes more. If it becomes too dry, add a little water or more tomatoes.

Note: If you want to make these tonight but don't have the sauce, substitute 3–4 teaspoons dry taco seasoning, ¼ cup water, and 2–3 teaspoons chipotle chile powder instead.

Want a yummy drink to go with your Baja pork? Muddle fresh mint, freshly squeezed lime juice, and a little agave nectar. Mix with carbonated mineral water and pour over ice. Crisp and refreshing!

Vegetable Spring Rolls

Homemade vegetable spring rolls are a great way to clear out the crisper. This recipe is a terrific base but can be expanded to bring in different veggies, flavor profiles, noodles, or other sources of protein. Look for wonton wrappers in the produce aisle. There are great served with the Asian Dipping Sauce on page 44.

MAKES 4 SPRING ROLLS

Ingredients:

2 teaspoons toasted sesame oil or vegetable oil

2 portabella mushrooms, stem and gills removed, sliced into strips

1 teaspoon garlic powder

4 cups shredded coleslaw mix

4 large egg roll wrappers

Pantry items:

Kosher salt

Water

Cooking spray

Directions:

In a medium skillet over medium-high heat, warm the oil. Add the mushrooms, garlic powder, and a large pinch of salt. Cook, stirring, until the mushrooms begin to release their juices, about 2 minutes. Add the coleslaw and cook until wilted, 3–5 minutes more. Remove from the heat and set aside until the mixture is cool enough to handle.

Place 1 wonton wrapper in front of you so that it looks like a diamond. Dip your finger in water and "paint" all the edges. Spoon ¼ of the cooled mixture across the middle of the wrapper. Take the corner closest to you and fold it over the mixture, 1½ inches from the top corner, and gently press it; it should resemble a triangle. Fold up the side corners toward the center. Starting with the bottom, firmly roll the wrapper toward the top, closing it. Set aside, seam down.

Once you have 3 spring rolls completed, preheat the air fryer to 320°F for 5 minutes.

Finish rolling the last spring roll. Lightly coat all of them with cooking spray and place them in the fry basket. Cook for 5 minutes. Rotate the rolls with tongs and cook an additional 5 minutes. Repeat in intervals of 2–3 minutes until the spring rolls are crispy all over.

Flatbread Veggie Pizzas

Take pizza night to the next level by having the family create their own healthy personal pizzas. Make them veggie lover or supreme!

MAKES 4 PIZZAS

Ingredients:

4 whole wheat tortillas (7 inches)

1 can (14.5 ounces) diced tomatoes with basil and garlic, drained

1 medium yellow squash, halved lengthwise and thinly sliced

¼ small red onion, thinly sliced

2 ounces crumbled goat cheese (plain or herbed)

Pantry items:

Cooking spray

Directions:

Preheat the air fryer to 360°F for 5 minutes.

Spray 1 side of a tortilla and place it in the fry basket, sprayed-side up. Cook for 5 minutes. Remove from the fryer and flip over onto a cutting board. Repeat for each tortilla.

While the tortillas are being prepped, combine the tomatoes, squash, and onion in a small bowl.

Spread ½ cup of the veggie mixture on each tortilla, leaving a ½-inch border. Crumble the goat cheese across the top. Place 1 pizza in the fry basket and cook until the tortilla is crispy and golden brown, 6–8 minutes. Repeat for each pizza.

Herb-Crusted Pork Chops

Serve these tangy chops with Sweet Potato Hash (page 74) and a side salad.

MAKES 2 SERVINGS

Ingredients:

¼ cup all-natural bran flake cereal, crushed

½ teaspoon dried thyme

2 bone-in pork chops (1-inch thick)

1–2 tablespoons Dijon mustard

Pantry items:

Kosher salt

Freshly ground black pepper

Metal rack (optional)

Cooking spray

Directions:

Preheat the air fryer to 360°F for 5 minutes.

Mix the bran flakes, thyme, and a large pinch of salt and pepper on a plate. Paint both sides of each pork chop with the mustard then press into the bran flakes, gently shaking off any excess crumbs.

Lightly coat the chops with cooking spray and place in the fry basket or on the metal rack, if desired. Lightly spray the tops. Cook for 15 minutes. Flip the chops, spray, and cook until the internal temperature reaches 145°F, 7–10 minutes more.

Simple Salmon with Pea Puree

If you have a habit of overcooking salmon, the air fryer is the perfect way to prepare it. This recipe is tried and true for no more dried-out fish! Choose thicker portions, not from the tail piece, which tend to be thinner. If you'd like to give another fish a try, arctic char makes for a great salmon substitute. For better flavor, opt for a mister of good-quality olive or grapeseed oil instead of regular cooking spray.

MAKES 2 SERVINGS

Ingredients:

For the salmon:
2 fillets (3–4 ounces each) wild-caught salmon, with or without skin
½ tablespoon butter, broken up into little chunks
2 lemon wedges

For the pea puree:
1 cup frozen baby sweet peas
½ tablespoon butter

Pantry items:

Cooking spray
Himalayan pink salt
Freshly ground black pepper
Water

Directions:

For the salmon: Preheat the air fryer to 390°F for 5 minutes. Spray the inside of the fry basket with cooking spray.

Sprinkle the flesh of the fish with a good pinch of salt and pepper. Place the fillets inside the fry basket and put the butter on top of each fillet.

Cook for 7 minutes and check on the fillets; they should be flaky and opaque. If they're not quite done enough, cook 1 minute more. Allow to rest with the machine turned off while you make the pea puree.

For the pea puree: In a small microwave-safe bowl, cook the peas with a splash of water, covered, on high until tender, about 1 minute. Transfer to a blender or food processor with the butter and a pinch of salt. Puree until smooth. (If you want it smoother, add 1 teaspoon water or a small splash of olive oil, and puree.)

To serve, dress a dinner plate with a generous smear of the pea puree, set a fillet skin-side down on top, and place a wedge of lemon on the side.

Crusted Pork Medallions with Rubbed Sage

Date night in can be just as fabulous as going to a fancy restaurant. Make this dish extra special and serve with roasted purple potatoes, Lemon-Pepper Green Beans (page 69), and a nice glass of sauvignon blanc. If you can't find pork medallions, slice them from a 1-pound pork tenderloin (freeze the other half).

MAKES 2 SERVINGS

Ingredients:
½ pound pork medallions (¾-inch thick)
3 tablespoons almond meal
1 teaspoon rubbed sage

Pantry items:
Kosher salt
Freshly ground black pepper
Metal rack (optional)
Cooking spray

Directions:
Preheat the air fryer to 320°F for 5 minutes. Season the medallions with salt and pepper on both sides.

Combine the almond meal and sage in a small bowl and coat both sides of each medallion.

Spray the medallions with cooking spray and place them in the fry basket or on a metal rack, if desired. Lightly spray the tops with cooking spray. Cook for 10 minutes. Remove the medallions and increase the temperature to 400°F.

Place the medallions back in the fry basket and lightly coat with cooking spray. Cook for 3–5 minutes. Flip the medallions, lightly coat with cooking spray, and cook until the pork reaches an internal temperature of 145°F and the coating is crispy, 3–5 minutes more.

Sriracha Shrimp

This fast, easy shrimp dish works great on its own or with a side of steamed veggies and brown rice. Or make extra shrimp and enjoy them on top of a salad with orange-sesame dressing and lots of crispy vegetables! For a slightly hot, sweeter variation, try this with Sriracha BBQ sauce. Look for wild-caught shrimp that's already been deveined and ready to go. If they're frozen, just thaw them in cool running water and pat dry before making the recipe.

MAKES 2 SERVINGS

Ingredients:
2 tablespoons Sriracha sauce (or to taste)
½ teaspoon garlic powder
16 medium-to-large wild-caught shrimp, peeled and deveined, tails removed

Pantry items:
Cooking spray

Directions:
Preheat the air fryer to 360°F for 5 minutes. Lightly coat the inside of the fry basket with cooking spray.

In a medium bowl, combine the Sriracha and garlic powder. Add the shrimp and toss to coat.

Place the shrimp in the fry basket and cook for 4 minutes. Toss the basket or turn the shrimp and cook until they are pink, firm, and curled, about 3 minutes more.

Serve immediately!

Jerk Tempeh with Toasted Coconut Cauli Rice

This Jamaica-inspired recipe displays tempeh's ability to take on many flavors. Pair it with Air-Fried Plantains with Avocado-Mango Relish (page 103) or Montego Bay Turnip Chips (page 104), and you'll be saying "Welcome to the island!" . . . kitchen island, that is. You can buy premade cauliflower rice in the produce section, but it's simple (and cheaper!) to make at home. Pop half a head's florets into a food processor and pulse until the pieces are about the size of long-grain rice.

MAKES 2 SERVINGS

Ingredients:
2 tablespoons Jamaican jerk seasoning

1 package (8 ounces) tempeh, sliced crosswise ¼-inch thick

2 cups cauliflower rice

½ cup unsweetened coconut milk beverage

¼ cup unsweetened coconut flakes

Pantry items:
Olive oil

Cake barrel

Kosher salt

Aluminum foil

Cooking spray

Directions:
Preheat the air fryer to 360°F for 5 minutes.

In a small bowl, combine the jerk seasoning with 3 tablespoons olive oil. Add the tempeh and gently toss to ensure each piece is nicely coated.

In the cake barrel, combine the cauliflower rice, coconut milk, coconut flakes, and a large pinch of salt. Cook for 5–7 minutes. Stir and cook until the rice is tender and the coconut is toasted, 7–10 minutes more. Remove the cake barrel and cover with aluminum foil or a plate to keep warm.

Lightly coat the fry basket with cooking spray and place the slices of tempeh in the basket. Cook until warmed through and the edges begin to crisp, 5–7 minutes. Serve with the rice.

Black Bean and Sweet Potato Burgers

This crowd-pleaser is sure to gain you some new fans. Double or triple the recipe and use in your weekly meal prep. (They freeze well, too! Fully thaw in the fridge then pop in the air fryer to cook.) Serve on whole wheat buns with lettuce, thick-cut tomato, and avocado. Top with a healthier Sriracha mayo using equal parts Greek yogurt and mayo, adding a little Sriracha to taste.

MAKES 4 BURGERS

Ingredients:
1 cup mashed cooked sweet potato

1 cup cooked brown rice

¾ cup rinsed-and-drained canned black beans (about ½ the can)

2 tablespoons taco seasoning

Pantry items:
Cooking spray

Directions:
Preheat the air fryer to 360°F for 5 minutes.

In a medium bowl, mix together the sweet potato, rice, beans, and taco seasoning until well combined. Divide the mixture into 4 equal portions and form into patties, about 4 inches wide.

Lightly coat with cooking spray and place 2 patties in the fry basket. Cook for 7 minutes. Flip and cook until firm to the touch and browned, 5–7 minutes more. Repeat for the remaining 2 patties.

Falafel Kebabs

This recipe easily transforms into patties for making pita sandwiches. Cook them in the fry basket until golden brown, about 5 minutes per side. Serve the falafel with tzatziki sauce.

MAKES ABOUT 12 FALAFEL

Ingredients:
1 can (15 ounces) chickpeas, drained and rinsed
1 handful flat-leaf parsley, coarsely chopped
¼ small red onion, chopped
½ teaspoon garlic powder

Pantry items:
Kosher salt
Freshly ground black pepper
Olive oil
4 skewers (see Note)
Multi-purpose skewer rack

Directions:
Preheat the fryer to 360°F for 5 minutes.

In a food processor, pulse together the chickpeas, parsley, onion, garlic powder, a large pinch of salt, and a pinch of pepper. With the motor running, add olive oil, 1 tablespoon at a time (up to 4 tablespoons), until the mixture becomes the consistency of crunchy peanut butter.

Spoon out about 2 tablespoons of the mixture and roll into a ball (wet your hands, if necessary, to prevent sticking). Set on a plate, and repeat until all the mixture has all been used.

Thread 3 falafel on each skewer. Set the skewers on the rack (put 3 on the rack and 1 directly on the fry basket beneath, if your rack has space for only 3 skewers). Cook for 10 minutes. Rotate the skewers and cook until the falafel begin to brown, 5 minutes more.

Note: Different brands of air fryer accessories come with differing numbers of skewers that their skewer racks can hold—from 3 to 6. Our versions hold 3, so adjust the recipe to suit the number of skewers your rack can hold. If you don't have the skewer rack, use 6½-inch wooden skewers, but soak them in water first to prevent them from burning, and set the skewers directly in the fry basket.

Turkey Koftas

Koftas are a type of meatball, often served on a skewer. Traditionally, they are made with lamb or a combination of beef and lamb, but this leaner turkey version will not leave you feeling cheated. Serve them with tzatziki sauce and a nice green salad.

MAKES 2 SERVINGS

Ingredients:

½ pound ground turkey

⅓ cup plain breadcrumbs

¼ onion, grated

2 tablespoons finely chopped flat-leaf parsley

1 teaspoon ground cumin

Pantry items:

Kosher salt

3 skewers (see Note) (6½-inches), soaked in water

Multi-purpose skewer rack

Directions:

Preheat the air fryer to 320°F for 5 minutes.

In a large bowl, mix together the turkey, breadcrumbs, onion, parsley, cumin, and a large pinch of salt until well combined. Divide the mixture into 6 equal portions and form into oval-shaped meatballs, 2 ½–3 inches x 1–1½ inches.

Thread 2 koftas on each skewer, leaving some space between each. Set the skewers on the rack and cook until the koftas are browned and an internal temperature reaches 165°F, 25–30 minutes. Remove the koftas from the skewers and divide between 2 plates.

Note: If you don't have the skewer rack, use 6½-inch wooden skewers, but soak them in water first to prevent them from burning, and set the skewers directly in the fry basket.

Summer Veggie Kebabs

With most veggies available year-round, this colorful recipe can give you a slice of summer, even in December.

MAKES 6 KEBABS

Ingredients:

12 grape or cherry tomatoes

1 large yellow bell pepper, cut into twelve 1-inch squares

1 medium zucchini, sliced into twelve ½-inch-thick rings

1 small or Japanese eggplant, cut into six 1 ¼-inch cubes

¼ cup Italian dressing

Pantry items:

6 skewers (see Note)

Multi-purpose skewer rack

Directions:

Place the tomatoes, bell pepper, zucchini, and eggplant in a medium bowl and add the Italian dressing. Mix until all the veggies are coated and marinate 5–10 minutes.

Preheat the air fryer to 360°F for 5 minutes.

Assemble the kebabs by threading the veggies onto each skewer in this order: tomato, bell pepper, zucchini, eggplant, zucchini, bell pepper, tomato. Place 3 kebabs on the rack and cook until the vegetables are tender and are browned around the edges, 6–9 minutes. Repeat with a second batch. Alternatively, place 2 rows of 3 kebabs each in the skewer basket and on the bottom of the fry basket and cook for 8–12 minutes.

Note: Different brands of air fryer accessories come with differing numbers of skewers that their skewer racks can hold—from 3 to 6. Our versions hold 3, so adjust the recipe to suit the number of skewers your rack can hold. If you don't have the skewer rack, use 6½-inch wooden skewers, but soak them in water first to prevent them from burning, and set the skewers directly in the fry basket.

Pistachio-Crusted Shrimp with Asian Dipping Sauce

This is a perfect meal starter for special guests, and the recipe easily doubles. The combination of sweet, spicy, and salty is heavenly! Look for wild-caught shrimp that are already deveined and ready to go. If they're frozen, just thaw them in cool running water and pat dry before making the recipe.

MAKES 4 KEBABS

Ingredients:

For the shrimp:
¾ cup roasted shelled pistachios
16 medium-to-large wild-caught shrimp, peeled and deveined, tails removed
1 or 2 large egg whites, whisked

For the dipping sauce:
2–3 tablespoons seasoned rice vinegar or ponzu sauce
1 clove garlic, minced (optional)
1 teaspoon coconut sugar
Pinch of crushed red pepper flakes
Sliced spring onion or scallion greens (optional)

Pantry items:

4 skewers (see Note)
Cooking spray
Multi-purpose skewer rack

Directions:

For the shrimp: In a food processor or blender, pulse the pistachios until they become breadcrumb consistency, but not too fine. Transfer to a plate.

With one hand, dip each shrimp fully into the egg whites, allowing excess to drip off. Hold it over the pistachios and use your other hand to sprinkle the pistachios all over it, instead of dipping it into the plate of pistachios. (This will keep the pistachios from getting wet and gooey.) Coat the shrimp entirely and thread it on a skewer. Repeat until all the shrimp are coated and skewered, allowing for a little space between the shrimp.

Preheat the air fryer to 360°F for 5 minutes.

Spray all sides of the shrimp with cooking spray and set the skewers on the rack. (If your rack holds only 3 skewers, set 1 on the bottom of the basket.) Place the rack in the fry basket and cook for 4 minutes. Turn the skewers and cook until the shrimp are pink, firm, and curled, about 3 minutes more.

Remove the shrimp from the skewers and serve with Asian Dipping Sauce.

For the dipping sauce: Place the vinegar or ponzu, garlic (if using), sugar, and red pepper flakes in a small microwave-safe dish and cook on high until the sugar has dissolved, 15 to 20 seconds. Stir to blend the ingredients, add the onion greens, if using, and serve immediately with the shrimp.

Note: Different brands of air fryer accessories come with differing numbers of skewers that their skewer racks can hold—from 3 to 6. Our versions hold 3, so adjust the recipe to suit the number of skewers your rack can hold. If you don't have the skewer rack, use 6½-inch wooden skewers, but soak them in water first to prevent them from burning, and set the skewers directly in the fry basket.

"N'awlins" Tofu

If a trip to the Big Easy is not in the plans, take a short walk to the kitchen and whip up these delicious vegan skewers, sip Hurricanes, and let the good times roll! For extra-crispy tofu, set the block on a couple paper towels on a plate, cover with more paper towels and another plate or cutting board, and set something heavy on top, like a can or skillet. Leave for 30 minutes. The pressing removes excess moisture from the tofu.

MAKES 2 OR 4 SERVINGS

Ingredients:

1 package (14 ounces) extra-firm tofu, drained, patted dry, halved, and cut into 8 equal strips

1½ teaspoons Creole seasoning

3 tablespoons garbanzo or whole wheat flour

½ cup aquafaba (the reserved liquid from 1 can of chickpeas)

1 heaping cup whole-grain cereal (can be corn, rice, or bran), crushed into small pieces

Pantry items:

8 skewers (see Note)

Cooking spray

Multi-purpose skewer rack

Directions:

On a plate, season the tofu strips with the Creole seasoning. Thread a skewer through each piece of tofu lengthwise and set aside.

Place the flour on a separate plate. Pour the aquafaba into a bowl or pie plate. Place the crushed cereal on another plate.

Preheat the air fryer to 360°F for 5 minutes.

Working with each skewer individually, cover all sides of the tofu with flour and tap off any excess. Dip all sides in the aquafaba, allowing excess to drip off, and cover in cereal. When all skewers have been coated, work in batches and spray with cooking spray on all sides.

Place the skewers on the rack and cook until golden brown and crispy, 10–12 minutes. Spray the remaining skewers with cooking spray and place on the rack. Cook for 10–12 minutes.

Note: Different brands of air fryer accessories come with differing numbers of skewers that their skewer racks can hold—from 3 to 6. Our versions hold 3, so adjust the recipe to suit the number of skewers your rack can hold. If you don't have the skewer rack, use 6½-inch wooden skewers, but soak them in water first to prevent them from burning, and set the skewers directly in the fry basket.

Moroccan Chicken Skewers

This succulent, easy chicken can be the base for any meal. It tastes great served with Roasted Stuffed Tomatoes (page 62) and brown rice or farro dusted with chopped pistachios, cinnamon, and a few raisins. We prefer free-range chickens for their superior taste and European-style yogurt for its thick consistency and nice tang.

MAKES 4 SKEWERS

Ingredients:

¼ cup European-style plain yogurt

2 tablespoons Moroccan seasoning

1 teaspoon freshly squeezed lemon juice + 2 lemon wedges

1 small clove garlic, minced (optional)

2 thinly sliced boneless, skinless chicken breasts (about 4 ounces each), cut into bite-size chunks

Pantry items:

Himalayan pink salt

4 skewers (see Note)

Cooking spray

Multi-purpose skewer rack

Directions:

In a small bowl or ziptop plastic bag, mix together the yogurt, Moroccan seasoning, lemon juice, garlic (if using), and a large pinch of salt. Add the chicken and stir (or close the bag and gently toss) to coat evenly. Cover and refrigerate for at least 1 hour (but it's even more succulent if you marinate overnight).

Remove the chicken from the refrigerator and allow it to rest at room temperature for 15–20 minutes. Preheat the air fryer to 390°F for 5 minutes.

Thread the pieces of chicken onto the skewers, leaving a bit of space between each piece. Continue until all the skewers are loaded. (Discard the marinade.) Lightly spray the skewers with cooking spray, place them on the rack, and set it inside the fry basket. (If your rack holds only 3 skewers, do them in batches.) Cook until the internal temperature of the chicken reaches 165°F, 8–10 minutes, turning halfway through, if desired. Serve with the lemon wedges.

Note: Different brands of air fryer accessories come with differing numbers of skewers that their skewer racks can hold—from 3 to 6. Our versions hold 3, so adjust the recipe to suit the number of skewers your rack can hold. If you don't have the skewer rack, use 6½-inch wooden skewers, but soak them in water first to prevent them from burning, and set the skewers directly in the fry basket.

Zesty Orange Rib-Eye Skewers

Ponzu sauce is a Japanese citrus dipping sauce; look for it in the Asian aisle of your supermarket. Find Valencia orange peel in the spice aisle, or substitute fresh thinly sliced kumquats or fresh orange zest for a brighter flavor. Serve these skewers with brown rice and a green salad.

MAKES 4 SERVINGS

Ingredients:

5 tablespoons lime ponzu sauce

4 teaspoons dried Valencia orange peel

1 tablespoon coconut sugar

12 ounces rib-eye steak, cut into bite-size pieces

1 red bell pepper, cut into bite-size pieces

Pantry items:

Himalayan pink salt

Freshly ground black pepper

Directions:

In a medium bowl or ziptop plastic bag, combine the ponzu, orange peel, coconut sugar, and a large pinch of salt and black pepper. Add the steak, coating thoroughly, and refrigerate for several hours (even better overnight).

Remove the meat from the refrigerator and allow it to rest at room temperature for 15–20 minutes. Preheat the air fryer to 400°F for 5 minutes.

Alternately thread the cubes of meat and the bell pepper onto the skewers. (Discard the marinade.) Place the rack into the fry basket and add the kebabs.

Cook until the beef begins to brown on the edges and is cooked to your liking, 5–7 minutes. Remove the meat and peppers from the skewers and divide between 4 plates.

Note: Different brands of air fryer accessories come with differing numbers of skewers that their skewer racks can hold—from 3 to 6. Our versions hold 3, so adjust the recipe to suit the number of skewers your rack can hold. If you don't have the skewer rack, use 6½-inch wooden skewers, but soak them in water first to prevent them from burning, and set the skewers directly in the fry basket.

Shish Kebabs

You'll feel like you're at a summer BBQ with these kings of Kebabs. To add a little more zip to your marinade, add a squeeze of lemon juice. If you can't find shish Kebab seasoning, try Moroccan seasoning or za'atar, which is a Middle Eastern spice blend available in the spice aisle of some supermarkets or in Middle Eastern markets.

MAKES 4 SERVINGS

Ingredients:

2 tablespoons traditional shish kebab seasoning (we like Spicely Organics)

1 small clove garlic, minced

12 ounces rib-eye steak, cut into bite-size pieces

½ pint grape tomatoes

1 small red onion, cut into bite-size pieces

Pantry items:

Olive oil

Himalayan pink salt

Freshly ground black pepper

3 skewers (see Note)

Multi-purpose skewer rack

Directions:

In a medium bowl or ziptop plastic bag, combine the shish kebab seasoning, garlic, and a pinch of salt and pepper with 2 tablespoons olive oil. Add the steak, coating thoroughly, and marinate at least 30 minutes or overnight (refrigerate if longer than 30 minutes).

Remove the meat from the refrigerator and allow it to rest at room temperature for 15–20 minutes. Preheat the air fryer to 400°F for 5 minutes.

Alternately thread the cubes of meat, tomatoes, and onion onto the skewers, leaving a little space in between. (Discard the marinade.) Place the rack into the fry basket and add the kebabs.

Cook until the beef begins to brown on the edges and is cooked to your liking, 5–7 minutes.

Note: Different brands of air fryer accessories come with differing numbers of skewers that their skewer racks can hold—from 3 to 6. Our versions hold 3, so adjust the recipe to suit the number of skewers your rack can hold. If you don't have the skewer rack, use 6½-inch wooden skewers, but soak them in water first to prevent them from burning, and set the skewers directly in the fry basket.

CHAPTER 3
Sides
(with Some Extra Love for the Sweet Potato)

Stuffed Cremini Mushrooms

Stuffed mushrooms are seriously delicious, and you'll want to make these for company. Have fun experimenting with fresh herbs from your summer garden too! For a different stuffing, try sliced basil mixed with mozzarella or herbed goat cheese and seasoned breadcrumbs. If you don't have almond meal, blend a few almonds in your food processor. Just don't grind them so fine that they become almond flour, which is too fine for this recipe and will become mushy.

MAKES 2 SERVINGS

Ingredients:

8 medium cremini mushrooms

3–4 tablespoons almond meal

Scant ½ teaspoon dry rubbed sage

2–3 tablespoons grated zucchini, excess moisture squeezed out

2 tablespoons freshly grated Parmesan cheese

Pantry items:

Olive oil

Himalayan pink salt

Freshly ground black pepper

Cooking spray

Directions:

Preheat the air fryer to 340°F for 5 minutes.

Rinse and pat dry the mushrooms. Trim the dry tip off the stems and discard. Remove the remaining stems and chop. Add to a small bowl along with the almond meal, sage, zucchini, and Parmesan. Gently toss and add a drizzle of olive oil and a pinch of salt and pepper. The consistency should be crumbly and moist but not wet.

With a spoon, add the mixture to the inside of each mushroom cap, mounding it over top.

Using tongs, carefully place the mushrooms into the fry basket. Lightly spray the tops of the mushrooms with cooking spray.

Cook until the mushrooms are tender, 9–10 minutes, checking once to make sure the tops are turning brown and not burning.

Easy Balsamic-Roasted Vegetables

To ensure the correct flavor, be sure to use balsamic glaze, not straight balsamic vinegar. Look for it in the Italian foods section of your supermarket or make your own reduction by gently simmering balsamic vinegar with a pinch of brown sugar until it reduces by half the amount. If making your own reduction, you can eliminate the olive oil in the recipe because the homemade reduction has more moisture than the store-bought version.

MAKES 2–4 SERVINGS

Ingredients:

1 tablespoon balsamic glaze

½ eggplant, cut into 1-inch cubes

1 red bell pepper, cut into 1-inch pieces

½ onion, cut into 1-inch pieces

1–2 tablespoons shaved Parmesan cheese

Pantry items:

Olive oil

Kosher salt

Freshly ground black pepper

Cake barrel

Directions:

Preheat the air fryer to 360°F for 5 minutes.

In a medium bowl, combine the balsamic glaze and 1 tablespoon olive oil. Add the eggplant, bell pepper, onion, and a good pinch of salt and black pepper. Toss until nicely coated.

Transfer the veggies to the cake barrel and cook for 7–10 minutes. Stir well, ensuring the vegetables on the bottom are rotated to the top of the pan, and cook until your desired tenderness, 5–7 minutes more. Garnish with Parmesan cheese.

Farro with Shaved Brussels Sprouts

Farro is truly a special ancient grain. Also called emmer, it's been grown for thousands of years, dating as far back as the ancient Egyptians. It's delicious and a good source of protein and fiber. Because it hasn't been hybridized like many other grains, it has retained a lot of nutrients and its robust taste. It's great in place of arborio rice in risotto or as an addition to cold salads in place of pasta. Only a handful of farmers grow this chewy, nutty grain worldwide. Support the farmers who are still growing this special crop.

MAKES 4 SERVINGS

Ingredients:
1 cup dry farro
3 cups vegetable broth
3 cups (12 ounces) medium brussels sprouts
½ tablespoon butter
2 ounces crumbled goat cheese

Pantry items:
Olive oil
Himalayan pink salt
Freshly ground black pepper
Cake barrel
Aluminum foil
Metal rack

Directions:
Cook the farro in the vegetable broth on the stove according to package instructions.

While the farro is cooking, preheat the air fryer to 360°F for 5 minutes.

Rinse and pat dry the brussels sprouts. Trim the stems and thinly slice the sprouts lengthwise. Toss in a medium bowl with a little olive oil, salt, and pepper. Stir to coat.

Transfer the sprouts to the cake barrel. Cover with aluminum foil and the metal rack to keep them from flying up into the heating element. Cook for 6–8 minutes. Stir the sprouts, replace the covers, and cook for another 5 minutes. Stir, cover, and cook until the brussels begin to soften but are still slightly crunchy, another 5 minutes.

In a serving bowl, gently combine the cooked farro and brussels sprouts with the butter and a pinch of salt and pepper. Add the crumbled goat cheese, stir gently, and serve immediately.

Roasted Stuffed Tomatoes

In summer, it seems as if everyone has an abundance of tomatoes popping off the vines. But there're only so many ways to eat them raw. Say no more, as roasting in the air fryer will keep you enjoying them all summer—without heating up your kitchen. If you have any leftover cooked farro from the previous recipe (page 61), toss it in too! Leftover tomatoes do not store well, so cook only as many as you wish to enjoy per meal. For best results, choose firm, round tomatoes that can sit level, without toppling over.

MAKES 4 SERVINGS

Ingredients:
4 medium vine-ripened tomatoes
1 cup shredded zucchini, squeezed to remove excess moisture
1 tablespoon grated red onion
¼ cup seasoned breadcrumbs
2 tablespoons shaved Parmesan cheese

Pantry items:
Olive oil
Himalayan pink salt
Fresh ground black pepper
Cooking spray
Chopped parsley, to garnish (optional)

Directions:
Preheat the air fryer to 360°F for 5 minutes.

Cut off the top ¼ inch from the tomatoes. With a spoon, scoop out the centers, discarding the jelly and seeds. Do not scoop all the way to the bottom; this will help it stay intact when cooked.

In a small bowl, lightly mix the zucchini, onion, breadcrumbs, and cheese. Add a drizzle of olive oil and a pinch of salt and pepper. Do not smash the ingredients; keep them loose.

Spoon the mixture into the tomatoes, mounding it over the top.

Spray the bottom of the fry basket with cooking spray. Carefully set the tomatoes inside and lightly spray the tops.

Cook until the tops are turning golden brown and/or the tomatoes are tender, 10 minutes. (For extra-crispy yummy bits, mix a bit more cheese and breadcrumbs together and sprinkle over the tops at the 8-minute mark, respray with cooking spray, and cook for the additional 2 minutes.)

Carefully remove the tomatoes with a large spoon or tongs and set on a plate. As they cool, the skins will begin to soften and crack, so it's best to serve immediately. Sprinkle with chopped parsley, if desired.

Buffalo Brussels Sprouts

Funny how certain vegetables come in vogue and show up in everyone's grocery cart. Well, that's good for all of us because brussels sprouts rock! These little beauties are super-satisfying with the bite of hot sauce—and the air fryer cooks them perfectly. We prefer the amazing, rich taste of Cholula hot sauce, but your favorite brand will work just as well.

MAKES 2–4 SERVINGS

Ingredients:

8 ounces medium brussels sprouts, trimmed and cut in half lengthwise

1 slice good-quality peppered bacon, cooked and crumbled

2 tablespoons hot sauce (or more, to taste)

2 tablespoons olive oil

Crumbled blue cheese, any variety (optional)

Pantry items:

Himalayan pink salt

Freshly ground black pepper

Cooking spray

Directions:

Preheat the air fryer to 400°F for 5 minutes.

In a large bowl, toss together the brussels sprouts, bacon, hot sauce, olive oil, and a good pinch of salt and pepper. Place directly in the fry basket.

Cook for 6–7 minutes. Open the air fryer and toss the brussels sprouts with a shake or two. Spray a little with cooking spray, and cook for another 6–7 minutes. Check on them and cook until the edges are brown and they're to your desired tenderness, another 2–3 minutes if necessary.

Sprinkle with blue cheese, if desired, and serve immediately.

Eggplant Bruschetta with Roasted Polenta

This recipe is sort of like a ratatouille. We're calling it "bruschetta" because it's great spread on good-quality, crusty whole-grain bread. To make this dish vegan, substitute nutritional yeast flakes for the Parmesan cheese. If you've never heard of nutritional yeast flakes before, look for them in the natural foods section (sometimes refrigerated) of your supermarket. It has a nutty and "cheesy" taste that's wonderful on eggs, popcorn, and roasted veggies.

MAKES 4 SERVINGS

Ingredients:

For the eggplant:

1 large eggplant, cut into bite-size cubes (about 3 cups)

½ can (14.5 ounces) fire-roasted diced tomatoes (with garlic and/or basil, if you can find it)

½ medium red onion, diced

2 cloves garlic, minced

2 tablespoons freshly sliced basil + more for garnish

For the polenta:

½ package (18 ounces) prepared polenta roll

Freshly grated Parmesan cheese

Pantry items:

Olive oil

Himalayan pink salt

Freshly ground black pepper

Cake barrel

Water

Cooking spray

Directions:

For the eggplant: Preheat the air fryer to 320°F for 5 minutes.

Place the eggplant in a large bowl, drizzle with olive oil, and add a healthy pinch of salt and pepper. Stir to coat.

Transfer the eggplant to the cake barrel and set it in the fry basket. Cook for 10 minutes. Add the tomatoes, onion, garlic, and ½ cup water. Cook for another 10 minutes. Stir, adding another ½ cup water, and cook for 5 minutes. Reduce the temperature to 260°F and cook until the eggplant is tender, 5–6 minutes more. If it looks too dry, add a little more water or tomatoes. Cooking times will vary depending on machine, but overall, this recipe should take about 30 minutes to cook. Transfer to a bowl and cover to keep warm while you prepare the polenta. Stir in the fresh basil before serving on top of sliced polenta. Sprinkle with more fresh basil for garnish.

For the polenta: Preheat the air fryer to 400°F.

Slice the polenta into ½-inch-thick discs. Spray with a little cooking spray and place them in the fry basket. Cook for 20 minutes and flip them over. Sprinkle with the cheese and spray with a little cooking spray (not too close or the cheese will fly around). Cook until the edges become crispy, 10 minutes more.

Lemon-Pepper Green Beans

Sometimes, all a perfect summer veggie needs is a simple decoration. It doesn't get much better than lemon and pepper for these green beans.

MAKES 4 SERVINGS

Ingredients:

1 pound green beans, trimmed

2 teaspoons olive oil

1 teaspoon lemon-pepper seasoning

Zest of ½ lemon, *divided* (optional)

Directions:

Preheat the air fryer to 360°F for 5 minutes.

In a medium bowl, combine the green beans, oil, lemon-pepper seasoning, and half of the zest, if using, and toss until the beans are evenly coated.

Transfer the beans to the fry basket and cook for 7–10 minutes. Stir and cook until your preferred level of tenderness, 2–3 minutes more, if necessary. Garnish with the remaining zest, if desired.

Asian Sweet Potato and Shrimp Crisps

These super-easy little bites are terrific for a side dish—but they're also great to enjoy with a crisp glass of vino on the back porch with friends. Make them ahead of time and simply reheat for a minute or two at 360°F to crisp up when company comes! If using frozen shrimp, thaw under cool running water before proceeding with the recipe.

MAKES ABOUT 8 CRISPS

Ingredients:

For the crisps:

1 medium-large sweet potato (about 12 ounces), peeled and grated

4 medium-to-large wild-caught shrimp, peeled and deveined

1 large egg

5 tablespoons whole wheat flour

For the dipping sauce:

¼ cup seasoned rice vinegar

2 teaspoons tamari or low-sodium soy sauce

1 teaspoons coconut sugar

1 clove garlic, minced

¼ teaspoon crushed red pepper flakes

Pantry items:

Water

Cooking spray

Directions:

For the crisps: In a medium bowl, mix the sweet potato with enough cold water to cover. Set aside for 30 minutes to allow excess starch to leach out.

Drain and squeeze the excess water out of the potato with your hands. Return the sweet potato to the bowl.

Preheat the air fry to 360°F for 5 minutes.

Cut the shrimp into small chunks (about 4 chunks per shrimp, depending on size). Pat dry with a paper towel.

In a small bowl, whisk the egg then mix in the flour until there are no lumps. And to the sweet potatoes and mix thoroughly with your hands until blended. Add the shrimp and thoroughly combine.

Spray the bottom of the fry basket with cooking spray. With clean hands, mound a 2-to-3-inch pile of the mixture in the bottom of the basket. Continue until the basket is full, leaving ½-inch space between mounds. (Cook in 2 batches if they don't all fit in your machine's basket.)

Spray the mounds with cooking spray and cook for 5 minutes. Turn them over and spray the other side. Cook until the crisps are firm and the loose pieces of sweet potato begin to brown, 5 minutes more. Make sure the shrimp is fully cooked and firm.

Serve warm with the dipping sauce.

For the dipping sauce: In a small saucepan over medium heat, combine the rice vinegar, tamari, coconut sugar, garlic, and pepper flakes and cook until the sugar is dissolved.

Crispy Cajun Sweet Potato Wedges

These wedges have just the right amount of heat. Pair with "N'awlins" Tofu (page 47), and you're on your way to a soul-food feast.

MAKES 2 SERVINGS

Ingredients:
1 small-medium sweet potato (about 8 ounces), peeled or not, cut lengthwise into 8 wedges

¼ cup almond meal

1 teaspoon Creole seasoning

Pantry items:
Water

Cooking spray

Directions:
Preheat the air fryer to 360°F for 5 minutes.

In a microwave-safe bowl, cook the sweet potato with 1 tablespoon water on high until tender, 3 minutes. Allow to cool.

On a plate, combine the almond meal and Creole seasoning. Spray a potato wedge with cooking spray then roll it in the almond meal mix, coating all sides. Shake off any excess mix and place it in the fry basket. Repeat with remaining wedges. Lightly coat the wedges with cooking spray.

Cook for 12–15 minutes. Flip the wedges and cook until lightly browned and crispy, 5–7 minutes more.

Sweet Potato Hash

This hash recipe is absolutely delicious and versatile. Serve it for breakfast with a fried egg or for dinner with Herb-Crusted Pork Chops (page 26). Yum!

MAKES 2–4 SERVINGS

Ingredients:

1 medium sweet potato, peeled and cut into ½-inch cubes

½ cup diced mixed-colored bell peppers

½ cup diced onion

Pantry items:

Olive oil

Kosher salt

Freshly ground black pepper

Directions:

Preheat the air fryer to 360°F for 5 minutes.

In a medium bowl, combine the sweet potato, bell peppers, onion, 1 tablespoon olive oil, and a pinch of salt and pepper. Mix until all the vegetables are well coated.

Transfer the veggies to the fry basket and cook for 10 minutes. Stir and cook for an additional 10 minutes. Check the tenderness of your sweet potatoes, and if additional time is needed, cook in intervals of 2–3 minutes more.

Curried Sweet Potato Fritters

This is one of our favorite recipes in the book. Try it, and you'll see why. We like them extra spicy, so we prefer Patak's hot curry paste. If you're new to curry paste, try a more mild yellow or green Thai curry paste. All are located in the Asian or Indian section of your supermarket.

MAKES 6–8 FRITTERS

Ingredients:

2 large eggs

2 tablespoons curry paste

1 medium sweet potato, peeled and grated (about 2 cups loosely packed)

½ cup whole wheat flour

½ cup frozen peas, thawed and patted dry

Pantry items:

Himalayan pink salt

Cayenne pepper

Cooking spray

Directions:

Preheat the air fryer to 400°F for 5 minutes.

In a medium bowl, whisk together the eggs and curry paste. Add the sweet potato and fold in with your hands to coat. Slowly mix in the flour and a pinch of salt and cayenne. Add the peas.

Spray the inside of the fry basket with cooking spray. Carefully place small mounds (scant ¼ cup) of the mixture evenly around the bottom of the basket. Spray the fritter mixture with cooking spray.

Cook 4 minutes. Turn the fritters over, spray them with cooking spray, and cook until they begin to brown on the edges, 4 minutes more.

Ancho Sweet Potato Strings

These little crispy bits work great on top of your favorite taco salad, soup, or chili. Or eat them straight as a good healthy-carb snack. If you don't have a vegetable spiralizer, look for prepackaged spiraled sweet potatoes in the produce department. To store any unused portion, place in a bowl with paper towel or a loose piece of parchment paper over top. Do not place in an airtight container or they will become soft.

MAKES 4 SERVINGS

Ingredients:
1 small Japanese or purple-skinned sweet potato, peeled (if desired) and spiralized
½–1 teaspoon ancho chile powder (to taste)

Pantry items:
Cooking spray
Himalayan pink salt

Directions:
Preheat the air fryer to 320°F for 5 minutes.

Place the sweet potato spirals in a medium bowl and spray with cooking spray. Add the chile powder and a large pinch of salt and toss to evenly coat.

Transfer the strings to the fry basket and cook for 4 minutes. Open and shake or stir the spirals. Cook until they become crisp, about 4 minutes more.

Remove from the fryer and add another hit of salt. Allow to cool.

CHAPTER 4
Snacks and Chips: No-Guilt Munchies for Any Time of Day

Garlic-Parmesan Chickpeas

Snacking is life, and chickpeas are both healthy and packed with protein. As a bonus, you can reserve the liquid from their can, or "aquafaba," for a vegan egg substitute (3 tablespoons per large egg and 2 tablespoons per large egg white). Or use it for Zucchini Soldiers (page 113) or "N'awlins" Tofu (page 47).

MAKES 2 SERVINGS

Ingredients:

1 can (15 ounces) chickpeas, drained, rinsed, and patted dry

1 tablespoon olive oil

1 tablespoon grated Parmesan cheese or vegan Parmesan sprinkle cheese

1 teaspoon garlic powder

1 teaspoon Italian seasoning

Pantry items:

Kosher salt

Directions:

Preheat the air fryer to 360°F for 5 minutes.

In a medium bowl, combine the chickpeas, olive oil, cheese, garlic powder, Italian seasoning, and a large pinch of salt.

Transfer the chickpeas to the fry basket and cook for 12 minutes. Stir and cook until crispy and golden, 3–5 minutes more. Depending on the amount of moisture, you may need to repeat this step in increments of 2–3 minutes.

Store in an airtight container for up to 5 days.

Roasted Garlic and Bean Dip

Go ahead and roast the whole garlic bulb! You can never go wrong adding roasted garlic to a dish. This dip is no exception. It's terrific with raw veggies.

MAKES 6–8 SERVINGS

Ingredients:

5–8 cloves garlic

2 teaspoons + ¼ cup olive oil, *divided*

1 can (15.5 ounces) white beans (cannellini or great Northern), drained and rinsed

1 teaspoon Italian seasoning

Squeeze of fresh lemon juice (optional)

Pantry items:

Kosher salt

Directions:

Preheat the air fryer to 360°F for 5 minutes.

In a small heat-proof dish or mixing bowl, combine the garlic and 2 teaspoons olive oil. Place in the fry basket and cook until the garlic is browned and tender, 10 minutes.

Allow to cool then remove the skins from the garlic. Place in a food processor with ¼ cup olive oil, the beans, Italian seasoning, a squeeze of lemon (if using), and a large pinch of salt. Process until smooth.

Roasted Beet Hummus

Serve this delicious pink hummus with sliced veggies or Everything Pita Chips (page 88), or use it as a spread on sandwiches in place of traditional condiments. When cooking beets, make sure you don't ditch the greens. They are said to have a higher iron content than spinach and are great sautéed with a little olive oil, salt, and a dash of balsamic vinegar.

MAKES 6–8 SERVINGS

Ingredients:
2 small beets, cut in half, leaves and stems removed
1 can (15 ounces) chickpeas, drained and rinsed
2 tablespoons tahini
2 cloves garlic
2 teaspoons fresh lemon juice

Pantry items:
Olive oil

Directions:
Preheat the air fryer to 360°F for 5 minutes.

In a small bowl, coat the beets with olive oil. Transfer the beets to the fry basket and cook until tender, 20 minutes.

Remove the beets from the basket and return to the bowl. Cover with plastic wrap and allow the beets to cool. Once cooled, peel the beets (discard the skins).

Place the beets in a food processor along with the chickpeas, tahini, garlic, lemon juice, and 6 tablespoons olive oil. Process until smooth, adding up to 2 additional tablespoons of olive oil, if needed for a smoother consistency. Refrigerate, covered, for at least 1 hour before serving.

Everything Pita Chips

Whole wheat pitas are the canvas on which you can paint until your heart is content. Go sweet or savory—the options are boundless. We like Papa Pita's Whole Wheat Greek Pita Flat Breads, but any pocket-style pita will work just as well. Look for everything-bagel spice at specialty food stores or online. Try these chips with Roasted Beet Hummus (page 87) or Roasted Garlic and Bean Dip (page 84).

MAKES 16 PITA CHIPS

Ingredients:

2 whole wheat pitas, cut into 8 wedges each

2 tablespoons everything-bagel spice

Pantry items:

Olive oil

Directions:

Preheat the air fryer to 360°F for 5 minutes.

Brush 1 side of each pita with olive oil and season with the bagel spice. Place seasoned-side down in the fry basket. Cook for 5 minutes. Flip over each chip and cook until crispy, 2–3 minutes more.

Sweet and Spicy Almonds

Warning: you cannot eat just 1 or 2 of these! You may as well just double the recipe. The coconut sugar adds a caramel brown sugar touch. Be sure to get chipotle chile powder, not regular chili powder; it adds a great level of flavor and heat. The two are a perfect marriage of sweet and spice.

MAKES 4 SERVINGS

Ingredients:

1 tablespoon coconut sugar

1½ teaspoons olive oil

½ teaspoon chipotle chile powder

1 cup unsalted almonds (roasted or raw)

Pantry items:

Himalayan pink salt

Water

Shallow baking pan

Parchment paper or aluminum foil

Directions:

Preheat the air fryer to 360°F for 5 minutes.

In a small bowl, combine the coconut sugar, olive oil, chile powder, a pinch of salt, and 1–2 teaspoons water. Add the almonds and stir to coat.

Transfer the almonds to the baking pan and set it in the bottom of the fry basket. Cook for 5–7 minutes, stirring halfway through. Cook until the liquid has become gooey and thick, another 2–3 minutes.

Carefully remove the baking pan from the basket and pour the almonds out onto parchment paper or aluminum foil to cool. As they cool, they will become more dry.

Parsnip Chips with Garam Masala

Shake, shake, shake . . . shake your parsnips! Don't knock 'em! This slightly sweet, often overlooked, root veggie makes excellent chips. The key to getting a crispy chip is shaking the basket every few minutes. Garam masala is an Indian spice blend that adds warmth to dishes; look for it in the spice aisle of your supermarket. If you're out of coconut oil, olive oil is a good alternative.

MAKES 2 SERVINGS

Ingredients:
2–4 teaspoons coconut oil, melted
1 teaspoon garam masala
2 medium, thick parsnips, peeled

Pantry items:
Mandolin or vegetable slicer
Kosher salt

Directions:
Preheat the air fryer to 360°F for 5 minutes.

Combine the coconut oil and garam masala in a medium bowl. Thinly slice the parsnips with the mandolin on the bias (slight slant) into the bowl. Toss the slices around, ensuring each side is coated. Add 1 or 2 pinches of salt.

Transfer the slices to the fry basket and cook for 5 minutes. Shake the basket and cook for an additional 3–5 minutes. Repeat these intervals until they're as crisp as you like.

Spiced Apple Chips

Maintain the shape of your apple chips by cooking them with the metal rack on top—it works perfectly! Tart Granny Smith apples are our favorite for this recipe, but any variety you like will work well.

MAKES ABOUT 8 CHIPS

Ingredients:

1 apple
1–2 teaspoons olive oil
½ teaspoon ground cinnamon
½ teaspoon ground cardamom

Pantry items:

Mandolin or vegetable slicer
Metal rack

Directions:

Preheat the air fryer to 375°F for 5 minutes.

Using your mandolin, thinly slice the apple crosswise. With a knife, remove the center core and seeds.

In a medium bowl, combine the olive oil, cinnamon, and cardamom. Add the apples and gently toss, ensuring both sides of the apple chips are coated.

Transfer the apples to the fry basket and cover with the metal rack so they don't fly up into the fan or heat element.

Cook for 5–7 minutes. Flip the chips, cover with the metal rack, and cook for an additional 4–5 minutes. Remove the rack and repeat in 2-minute intervals until they're as crisp as you like.

Polenta Fries

These fries are a great snack and especially easy if you have polenta left over from Eggplant Bruschetta with Roasted Polenta (page 66). Serve with prepared pesto or marinara sauce.

MAKES 12–15 FRIES

Ingredients:

¼ package (18 ounces) prepared polenta roll

2 tablespoons freshly grated Parmesan cheese (or try Asiago for a stronger flavor)

¾ teaspoon Italian seasoning

Pantry items:

Cooking spray

Kosher salt

Directions:

Preheat the air fryer to 360°F for 5 minutes.

Cut the polenta into ½-inch-thick fries. Lightly coat them with cooking spray. Sprinkle with the cheese, Italian seasoning, and a pinch of salt.

Place the fries in the fry basket and cook until slightly golden on the edges, 10–15 minutes.

Chipotle Rutabaga Chips

Make sure there is no food-grade wax on the outside of the rutabagas. If so, remove it with a vegetable peeler, rinse, then pat dry. Also, if you can't find rutabagas that are smaller than your mandolin, cut them in half before slicing them.

MAKES ABOUT 3½ CUPS

Ingredients:

2 medium rutabagas, rinsed and peeled (halved, if necessary)
2–3 tablespoons olive oil
½ teaspoon chipotle chile powder
1 dash garlic powder

Pantry items:

Mandolin or vegetable slicer
Himalayan pink salt
Cooking spray
Parchment paper

Directions:

Preheat the air fryer to 400°F for 5 minutes.

Using the mandolin, carefully slice the rutabagas into thin chips.

In a medium bowl, combine the olive oil, chile powder, garlic powder, and a large pinch of salt. Add the rutabaga chips, turning by hand to make sure they are evenly coated on both sides.

Reduce the air fry temperature to 300°F. Spray the interior of the fry basket with cooking spray and put a loose handful of chips on the bottom. Cook for 5 minutes. Pull out the basket and give the chips a shake. Cook an additional 2–3 minutes. Repeat this step 2 or 3 times until the chips begin to brown on the edges. (Cook times will vary depending on the machine, and how many chips you have cooking in the basket at one time.)

Once done, pour out the chips onto parchment paper and allow to cool before eating.

Repeat to cook the remaining batches of chips.

Chili-Lime Taro Chips

Maybe you've heard of the elephant ear plant. Well, taro is its root. Though it's a staple in many tropical island nations, the taro root can look pretty intimidating. Once peeled and cooked, it becomes a delicious mineral- and vitamin-rich vegetable with about 3 times the amount of fiber as in a potato. Try it mashed like potatoes too! Be sure to enjoy it fully cooked as it is toxic raw.

MAKES ABOUT 2 CUPS

Ingredients:
6–7 inches taro root, peeled
2–3 tablespoons olive oil
Juice of ½ lime
2 teaspoons chili powder

Pantry items:
Mandolin or vegetable slicer
Himalayan pink salt

Directions:
Preheat the air fryer to 300°F for 5 minutes.

Thinly slice the taro using the mandolin.

In a medium bowl, whisk together the olive oil, lime juice, chili powder, and a large pinch of salt. Add the taro chips and coat each with the mixture.

Transfer the chips to the fry basket. Cook in 5-minute intervals, shaking the basket between cook times, until the chips are as crispy as you like them. If desired, add a pinch more salt and a hit of lime juice, to taste.

Air-Fried Plantains with Avocado-Mango Relish

We like to think of plantains as the banana's amazing big cousin; they're not quite as sweet, but they make fantastic chips. Look for mostly brown ones with some yellow on the peel. We're suggesting Ataulfo (or champagne) mangos, which are the smaller yellow ones. They are creamy and have less fibrous centers with a much smaller flat seed inside—which means more fruit, even though they are small!

MAKES 12–20 CHIPS

Ingredients:

For the plantains:
1 ripe plantain, peeled and sliced ¼-inch thick
¼–½ teaspoon ground allspice

For the relish:
1 ripe avocado, cubed
1 ripe Ataulfo (champagne) mango, cubed
¼ cup diced red bell pepper

Pantry items:
Olive oil
Squeeze of lemon or lime (optional)

Directions:
For the plantains: Preheat the air fryer to 360°F for 5 minutes.

In a medium bowl, lightly drizzle the plantain slices with olive oil. Toss to coat each side and sprinkle with the allspice.

Transfer the plantain chips to the fry basket and cook for 10 minutes. Flip and cook until crisp and beginning to brown, 3–5 minutes more. If you prefer a more caramelized plantain, extend the cook time by a few minutes.

For the relish: In a small bowl, gently mix the avocado, mango, and bell pepper. If you have a lime or any citrus, feel free to add a squeeze. Spoon on top of the fried plantain and enjoy at room temperature. (Use any leftover relish on the rutabaga chips on page 99 or the taro chips on page 100.)

Montego Bay Turnip Chips

Make sure there is no food-grade wax on the outside of your turnips. If so, remove it with a vegetable peeler, rinse, then pat dry. Also, make sure you get turnips that are not wider than your mandolin; otherwise, it will be hard to slice them.

MAKES ABOUT 3½ CUPS

Ingredients:
2 medium turnips, scrubbed and patted dry
½ teaspoon ground allspice
½ teaspoon ground ginger
¼ teaspoon ground cinnamon
¼ teaspoon crushed red pepper flakes

Pantry items:
Mandolin or vegetable slicer
Cooking spray
Garlic powder
Himalayan pink salt
Parchment paper

Directions:
Preheat the air fryer to 400°F for 5 minutes.

Using the mandolin, carefully slice the turnips into thin chips. Place in a medium bowl and spray with cooking spray.

In a small bowl, combine the allspice, ginger, cinnamon, red pepper flakes, and a pinch of garlic powder and salt. Sprinkle on the turnip chips, tossing them several times with your hands to coat them with the seasoning.

Reduce the air fryer temperature to 300°F. Spray the interior of the fry basket with cooking spray and add a loose handful of chips to the bottom. Cook for 5 minutes. Pull out the basket and give the chips a shake. Cook an additional 2–3 minutes. Repeat this step 2 or 3 times until the chips begin to brown on the edges. (Cook times will vary depending on the machine, and how many chips you have cooking in the basket at one time.)

Once done, pour out the chips onto parchment paper and allow to cool before eating.

Repeat to cook the remaining batches of chips.

CHAPTER 5
Kid-Friendly Foods: Tempting Treats for Even the Pickiest of Eaters

Vegan Taquitos

Kids love finger foods, and these taquitos are a great way to "sneak" in vegetables for picky eaters. Modify the recipe with ½ cup black beans and ½ cup finely chopped kale, if desired. Serve with salsa and guacamole.

MAKES 8 TAQUITOS

Ingredients:
¾ cup drained-and-rinsed canned black beans
¼ cup cooked brown rice
¼ cup vegan shredded cheddar cheese
½ teaspoon taco seasoning
8 corn tortillas

Pantry items:
Cooking spray
Water

Directions:
Preheat the air fryer to 360°F for 5 minutes. Lightly coat the fry basket with cooking spray.

In a medium bowl, combine the beans, rice, cheese, and taco seasoning. Add water, 1 tablespoon at a time, until the mixture binds together.

Warm the tortillas in the microwave according to package directions, about 30 seconds. One by one, place 2–3 tablespoons of the bean mixture into the center of each tortilla and roll it up. Place the taquitos snuggly into the fry basket.

Spray with a light coating of cooking spray and cook for 10 minutes.

Turn each taquito and apply another light coating of cooking spray. Cook until crispy and golden brown, 5–8 minutes.

Italian Quesadillas

These quesadillas are a delicious way to enjoy an abundance of squash and spinach—especially if the kids help pick them from the garden! Try various types of cheeses, like fontina or Asiago, for a bolder flavor. Serve with marinara sauce for dipping.

MAKES 2 QUESADILLAS

Ingredients:

½ cup shredded mozzarella cheese

2 whole wheat tortillas (8 inches)

About 20 fresh spinach leaves

1 small-to-medium yellow squash, halved lengthwise then cut into thin discs

2 cremini mushrooms, thinly sliced

Pantry items:

Cooking spray

Metal rack

Directions:

Preheat the air fryer to 360°F for 5 minutes.

Sprinkle 2 tablespoons of the cheese on half of 1 tortilla. Place half of the spinach leaves, squash, and mushrooms on the cheese, and sprinkle 2 tablespoons more cheese on top. Fold the tortilla over and spray with cooking spray.

Place the quesadilla in the fry basket and weigh down with the metal rack. Cook until the cheese melts and the edges are crisp, 5–7 minutes. Repeat with the remaining ingredients. Cut into wedges and serve.

Zucchini Soldiers

Using garbanzo flour instead of wheat flour adds fiber and protein to this snack. You can find it in the natural foods section of your grocery store or online. For a nuttier crunch, try crushed whole-grain cereals in place of the breadcrumbs. Serve these "soldiers" with ranch dressing for dipping. If you don't have seasoned breadcrumbs on hand, mix in 1 teaspoon Italian seasoning.

MAKES 4–6 SERVINGS

Ingredients:

3 tablespoons garbanzo or whole wheat flour

½ cup aquafaba (the reserved liquid from 1 can of chickpeas) or 1 egg + 1–2 tablespoons water

½ cup seasoned breadcrumbs

1 medium zucchini, cut into 3-inch x ½-inch sticks

Pantry items:

Kosher salt

Cookie sheet

Cooking spray

Directions:

Preheat the air fryer to 360°F for 5 minutes.

Place the flour on a plate. In a bowl, pour in the aquafaba or mix the eggs and water with a fork. On a second plate, mix the breadcrumbs with a pinch of salt.

Coat each zucchini stick with the flour, then the aquafaba or egg, and lastly the breadcrumbs. Lay fully breaded sticks on a cookie sheet.

Spray all the sticks with cooking spray and place them, sprayed-side down, in the fry basket. Spray the top of the zucchini sticks and cook for 10 minutes. Flip the sticks over and cook until crispy and golden brown, 7–10 minutes more.

Granola Wedges

Roll up the kids' sleeves and let them get their hands messy mixing in their favorite ingredients, from dried cranberries or goji berries to mini chocolate chips! These wedges are great served with yogurt.

MAKES 8 WEDGES

Ingredients:

1 cup quick oats

¼ cup slivered almonds

¼ cup raisins

¼ cup unsweetened applesauce

1 tablespoon agave nectar or raw honey

Pantry items:

Ground cinnamon

Shallow baking pan

Aluminum foil

Directions:

Preheat the air fryer to 360°F for 5 minutes.

In a medium bowl, combine the oats, almonds, raisins, and a pinch of cinnamon. Add in the applesauce and agave or honey and mix well.

Press the mixture firmly into the baking pan, ensuring the mix is even. Cover with aluminum foil. Cook for 15 minutes. Remove the foil and cook until lightly golden brown, 3–5 minutes more.

Carefully remove the baking pan from the fryer and cool completely. Turn out the granola onto a cutting board and cut into 8 wedges before serving.

Mini Corn Pups

Who says you have to go to the county fair to enjoy a corn dog? We've made these little "pups" vegan for your little one. Serve them with your kids' favorite condiments. Look for the dogs in the refrigerated natural foods section of your grocery store. We especially like Simple Truth Organic Gluten-Free Cornbread Baking Mix because not only because it's organic but also because it's vegan straight out of the box. If it's not in a store near you, look for it online.

MAKES 12 MINI PUPS

Ingredients:
½ box Simple Truth Organic Cornbread Mix

½ cup nondairy or dairy milk

2½ tablespoons vegetable oil

2 tablespoons unsweetened applesauce

2 vegetarian or uncured frankfurters, each cut into 6 pieces

Pantry items:
Mini silicone cupcake pan

Directions:
Preheat the air fryer to 360°F for 5 minutes.

In a medium bowl, mix together the cornbread mix, milk, oil, and applesauce until well combined.

Spoon 1 tablespoon of the cornbread mixture into each muffin cup. Place a frankfurter piece in the center and top with 1 more tablespoon of cornbread mixture.

Cook until a toothpick inserted down the side of one comes out clean and the tops are golden brown, 15–17 minutes. Allow to cool before removing and repeating with the remaining ingredients.

Veggie and Chickpea Nuggets

That's right—chickpea, not chicken! Those picky eaters won't know what hit them! Serve with your kids' favorite dipping sauce. Many supermarkets carry riced veggies in their produce section, but they're often pricey. Instead, pop a crown of broccoli into a food processor and pulse until the pieces are about the size of long-grain rice.

MAKES 14–18 NUGGETS

Ingredients:

¼ cup shredded carrots

¼ cup riced fresh broccoli

1 can (15 ounces) chickpeas, drained and rinsed

¼ cup unsweetened applesauce

½ cup panko breadcrumbs

Pantry items:

Water

Garlic powder

Kosher salt

Cookie sheet

Cooking spray

Directions:

Place the carrots, broccoli, and 1 tablespoon water in a microwave-safe bowl. Cover with a paper towel and cook on high until tender, 1 minute.

Place the chickpeas in a food processor and pulse until they're chopped up into smaller pieces. Add the carrots, broccoli, applesauce, 2 large pinches of garlic powder, and a large pinch of salt. Blend until the mixture comes together (you should still see bits of the vegetables and chickpeas).

Preheat the air fryer to 360°F for 5 minutes.

Pour the panko on 1 side of the cookie sheet. Using an ice cream scoop, portion out each nugget and press into small patties. Coat each nugget with the panko and place on the clean side of the cookie sheet.

Once all the nuggets have been coated, place half of them in the fry basket and spray with cooking spray. Cook for 10 minutes. Flip the nuggets over and spray with cooking spray. Cook until crispy and golden brown, 3–5 minutes more. Repeat with remaining nuggets.

BBQ Tempeh Sticks

Tempeh is a good source of plant-based protein. It has a chewy texture to satisfy folks who enjoy something heartier than tofu; dress it up with various sauces, and try it in stir-fries. Tempeh is minimally processed using fermented soybeans, which add vitamins, minerals, and probiotics. Look for non-GMO varieties in the refrigerated section of the natural foods aisle. Also choose a BBQ sauce that does not contain high fructose corn syrup. Serve these sticks with fresh veggies or a favorite side.

MAKES 4 SERVINGS

Ingredients:

1 package (8 ounces) tempeh, cut crosswise into 8–12 sticks

½ cup all-natural BBQ sauce

Directions:

Place the tempeh in a medium bowl. Pour over the BBQ sauce, ensuring each piece is coated. (If using a thicker sauce, thin a bit with water first.) Cover and let the sticks marinate at room temperature for 30 minutes.

Preheat the air fryer to 360°F for 5 minutes.

Transfer the sticks to the fry basket. Cook until warmed through and browned, 8–10 minutes.

Grilled Cheese and Grilled PBB Sandwiches

Take lunchtime up a notch and toast up these childhood favorites. Serve them with yogurt or unsweetened applesauce.

MAKES 4 WEDGES

Ingredients:

2 slices cheese (choose your favorite)

4 slices whole wheat bread, *divided*

2 tablespoons room temperature butter, *divided*

4 tablespoons peanut butter

1 banana

Directions:

Preheat the air fryer to 360°F for 5 minutes.

Place the cheese slices between 2 slices of bread. Butter each side of the sandwich.

Spread the peanut butter on the remaining 2 slices of bread. Cut the banana in half crosswise and slice each half into 3 strips. Layer the banana slices on top of the peanut butter on 1 slice and top with the other slice of bread. Butter each side of the sandwich.

Place the sandwiches in the fry basket and cook until golden, 3–5 minutes on each side. Cut in half before serving.

Broccoli Tots

A tot for your tot! Have fun making these with your tiny sous chef—just make sure you add a little cooking oil to their hands first. They will enjoy getting a little messy with you! Serve the tots with ketchup or BBQ Tempeh Sticks (page 121).

MAKES 2–4 SERVINGS

Ingredients:

2 cups riced broccoli (fresh, frozen, or homemade—see page 118)

1½ teaspoons garlic powder or onion powder

⅓ cup shredded mild cheddar cheese

1 large egg

⅔ cup plain breadcrumbs

Pantry items:

Water

Olive oil

Kosher salt

Directions:

Preheat the air fryer to 360°F for 5 minutes.

Place the broccoli and 2 tablespoons water in a microwave-safe bowl. Cover with a paper towel and cook on high until tender, 1 minute. Sprinkle with the garlic or onion powder and a pinch of salt and set aside to cool a bit.

Stir in the cheese and egg and mix well. Stir in the breadcrumbs, a bit at a time, until well incorporated.

Rub a bit of olive oil on your hands. Form 1½ tablespoons of the mixture into a "tot" and set on a plate. Repeat until all the tots have been formed, then place them in the fry basket. Cook until golden brown, 12–16 minutes.

CHAPTER 6
The Sweet Spot: Guilt-Free Desserts to Satisfy Your Sweet Tooth

Banana-Coconut Rolls

One of my favorite desserts at Asian restaurants is the banana egg roll, but I rarely order it because it's deep fried and too greasy. This recipe allows me to enjoy one of my faves without all of the guilt (though I do have them with a scoop of vanilla bean–almond ice cream and drizzled with chocolate!). The recipe is easily doubled or tripled.

MAKES 4 ROLLS

Ingredients:
2–3 tablespoons unsweetened coconut milk beverage
¼ cup shredded unsweetened coconut
4 large wonton wrappers
2 bananas, cut in half crosswise (try to avoid the overly curved ones)

Pantry items:
Water
Cooking spray

Directions:
Preheat the air fryer to 320°F for 5 minutes.

Place the coconut milk and coconut shreds in separate bowls.

Place 1 wonton wrapper in front of you so that it looks like a diamond. Dip a banana half in the coconut milk, allowing excess to drip off. Roll it in the coconut shreds and place it in the middle of the wrapper, crosswise.

Dip your finger in the water and "paint" all the edges of the wrapper. Take the corner closest to you and fold it over the banana, 1½ inches from the top corner, and gently press it; it should resemble a triangle. Fold up the side corners toward the center. Starting with the bottom, firmly roll the wrapper toward the top to close it. Set on a plate, seam down. Repeat for the remaining 3 banana halves.

Lightly coat the rolls with cooking spray and place in the fry basket. Cook for 8 minutes. Flip the rolls and cook until crispy, about 8 minutes more. Serve immediately.

Blackberry Cheesecake Chimichangas

We've turned the idea of cheesecake inside out. Instead of a buttery graham cracker crust, mounds of sugar, and a sour cream topping, we keep what's delicious about this dessert—the cream cheese—and wrap it in a whole wheat tortilla. This recipe is just as delicious if you choose to make it with vegan cream cheese and butter.

MAKES 4 CHIMICHANGAS

Ingredients:

1 package (8 ounces) cream cheese or Neufchâtel, room temperature

3 tablespoons coconut sugar, *divided*

1 cup blackberries, halved

4 whole wheat tortillas (8 inches)

1 tablespoon butter, melted (optional)

Pantry items:

Cooking spray, optional

Directions:

In a medium bowl with a hand mixer, combine the cream cheese and 2 tablespoons of the sugar until well incorporated and fluffy, about 2 minutes. Gently fold in the blackberries.

Preheat the air fryer to 360°F for 5 minutes.

Take a tortilla and spread ¼ of the cheesecake mixture along the bottom third (the part closest to you). Roll up the side closest to you to just over the mix, fold in the right and left sides, then finish rolling up and set aside with the seam down.

Once all 4 chimichangas have been wrapped, brush the tops with the butter (or spray with cooking spray) and sprinkle with the remaining 1 tablespoon sugar. Place them in the fry basket and cook until the tortillas are golden brown and begin to crisp, 8–10 minutes.

Allow to cool for a couple of minutes before eating, as the cheesecake filling will be very hot.

Pear-Kumquat Tart

There's just something so special about the citrusy kumquat that packs such tartness in that little fruit. Try them here, or wherever recipes call for orange zest, to brighten any dish. With pear, it's a perfect marriage of sweet and bright that's sure to satisfy. If kumquats aren't in season, substitute with 2–3 tablespoons dried cranberries. Traditional tarts have crusts that are loaded with butter, and they're often topped with whipped cream. This version slims down by slashing the fat. Serve with a dollop of plain European-style yogurt or labne (yogurt cheese).

MAKES 4 SERVINGS

Ingredients:

1 tablespoon butter, *divided*

1 whole wheat or whole-grain tortilla (8 inches)

1 red pear (slightly firm is okay), or 2 Forelle pears

1 or 2 kumquats

2 teaspoons coconut sugar

Pantry items:

Cooking spray

Aluminum foil

Metal rack

Mandolin or vegetable slicer

Ground cinnamon

Ground cardamom (optional)

Directions:

Preheat the air fryer to 260°F for 5 minutes. Lightly spray the inside of the fry basket with cooking spray.

Cut 2 narrow pieces of aluminum foil about 14 inches long. Crisscross them and carefully place them in the machine to use as handles to pick up the tortilla once cooked.

Rub a small dollop of the butter on 1 side of the tortilla and place it, butter-side up, on top of the aluminum foil. Place the metal rack on top to prevent the fan from moving the tortilla while cooking.

Cook for 8–10 minutes.

While the tortilla is cooking, slice the pear in half lengthwise and remove the center with the seeds. Cut into thin wedges.

Using the mandolin, carefully slice the kumquat(s) paper thin.

In a medium skillet over medium-high heat, melt the remaining butter. Add the pear and kumquat(s) and cook, stirring, for 2 minutes. Sprinkle in a few dashes of cinnamon and a dash of cardamom, if desired, and stir to evenly coat the fruit. Turn off the heat and set aside, allowing the oils from the kumquat to infuse with the pear.

Open the air fryer and remove the metal rack. Spread the pear mixture on top of the tortilla. Sprinkle with the coconut sugar. Replace the rack and cook until the coconut sugar has melted, 2 minutes more.

Carefully remove the tart with the foil handles and set on a cutting board to cool slightly. Serve whole or cut into quarters.

Best-Ever 5-Ingredient Air Fryer Chocolate Cake

Sometimes it is best to start off with dessert because there won't be room for it at the end of your meal. What better way than with chocolate cake? This rich chocolate cake has no added sugar. With the simple chocolate glaze, it's sure to be a crowd-pleaser. Serve it with fresh berries.

MAKES 6 SERVINGS

Ingredients:

For the cake:

¼ cup coconut flour

½ teaspoon baking powder

4 tablespoons butter

¼ cup chocolate chips

3 large eggs, room temperature

For the glaze:

3 tablespoons butter

¼ cup chocolate chips

Pantry items:

Cake barrel

Cooking spray

Parchment paper

Kosher salt

Aluminum foil

Directions:

For the cake: Preheat the air fryer to 360°F for 5 minutes. Prepare the cake barrel by coating it with cooking spray. Cut the parchment paper into 4-inch-wide strips long enough to line the bottom of the barrel in an X pattern (this will help remove the cake when it's done).

In a small bowl, combine the coconut flour, baking powder, and a pinch of salt and set aside.

In a medium microwave-safe bowl, heat the butter until melted, 25–45 seconds. Add the chocolate chips and whisk until smooth and slightly cooler. Whisk in the eggs until well incorporated. Add the dry ingredients and mix until completely combined.

Pour the cake batter into the cake barrel and cover with aluminum foil. Cook for 40–45 minutes. Carefully uncover the cake and cook until a toothpick inserted into the center comes out clean, 3–5 minutes more.

Remove the fry basket and allow the cake to cool completely before removing the cake barrel. Use the parchment strips to help lift out the cake. Remove the parchment paper and set the cake on a plate (no need to flip).

For the glaze: In a small microwave-safe bowl, heat the butter on high until melted, 25–45 seconds. Add the chocolate chips and whisk until smooth. Using a spatula or butter knife, smooth the glaze evenly across the top of the cake. Allow to set before serving.

Strawberry Crisp

Did you know that strawberries aren't technically berries since their seeds are on the outside? In fact, they are part of the rose family. That might explain why they are so fragrant. Choose smaller berries, rather than those mammoth ones that require 3 or 4 bites, for a sweeter taste. The use of coconut sugar and flour make this crisp a bit more healthful than your typical dessert.

MAKES 4 SERVINGS

Ingredients:

1 pound strawberries, hulled and chopped (about 3 cups)

3 tablespoons coconut sugar, *divided*

½ cup quick oats

2 tablespoons coconut flour

5 tablespoons butter

Pantry items:

Cake barrel

Cooking spray

Water

Aluminum foil

Directions:

Preheat the air fryer to 360°F for 5 minutes. Spray the cake barrel with cooking spray.

Put the strawberries in the barrel and mix in 1 tablespoon of the coconut sugar and 1–2 teaspoons water.

In a medium bowl, combine the oats, coconut flour, and remaining 2 tablespoons coconut sugar. Using a fork, cut in the butter and mix until large crumbles form. Sprinkle the crumble topping over the strawberries.

Cover with foil and cook for 30 minutes. Carefully remove the foil and cook until the topping is golden brown, 5–8 minutes more.

Apple Galette

A galette is like a pie without a top crust. It's actually a perfect dessert for the air fryer because a tortilla can stand in for the crispy bottom crust, saving a lot of fat and calories. Be sure to make 2, because 1 is simply not enough to share. Serve warm or at room temperature with a scoop of vanilla ice cream.

MAKES 2 SERVINGS

Ingredients:

2 tablespoons butter, melted

½ teaspoon ground cinnamon

2 whole wheat tortillas (7 inches)

4 teaspoons coconut sugar, *divided*

1 Granny Smith apple, peeled and thinly sliced

Pantry items:

Shallow baking pan

Aluminum foil

Directions:

Preheat the air fryer to 320°F for 5 minutes.

In a small bowl, mix together the butter and cinnamon. Place 1 tortilla in the baking pan and gently push down to fit snugly.

Spread 1½ teaspoons of the butter mixture on the tortilla. Sprinkle 1 teaspoon of the coconut sugar on the tortilla. Layer half of the apple slices around the outer edge of the pie tin, slightly overlaying each slice (this will leave a small circle in the middle). Take 2 slices, finely chop them, and place in the center of the galette. Gently brush 1½ teaspoons of the butter mixture on top of the apple slices and evenly sprinkle with 1 teaspoon of the coconut sugar.

Cover with aluminum foil and cook for 7 minutes. Carefully remove the foil and cook until the apples caramelize on top, 7–10 minutes more. Remove the baking pan with tongs and lift the galette out with a spatula. Now get the second one cooked!

Gingered Almond Cookies

These low-sugar, gluten-free cookies are a perfect accompaniment for that afternoon cup of coffee. With the protein from the almond meal and the peppery spice from the ginger, they'll give you a boost. Some sources say ginger aids in fighting inflammation and helps immune function.

MAKES 14–16 COOKIES

Ingredients:

½ cup butter, melted and cooled

1 large egg

½ teaspoon vanilla extract

2¼ cups almond meal

¾ cup + 2 tablespoons crystalized ginger, chopped, *divided*

Pantry items:

Cooking spray

Parchment paper or cooling rack

Directions:

Preheat the air fryer to 350° for 5 minutes. Lightly spray the fry basket with cooking spray.

In a medium bowl, whisk together the cooled butter, egg, and vanilla. Slowly add in the almond meal until well blended. Toss in ¾ cup ginger.

Take about 2 tablespoons of dough and roll it in your palms and slightly flatten it. Place it in the basket and continue adding cookies, placing them ½ inch apart. Top each with a piece of ginger.

Cook until the cookies are slightly golden and crispy on the bottom, 8–10 minutes. Remove to parchment paper or a cooling rack to cool while you cook the second batch.

Conversion Charts

METRIC AND IMPERIAL CONVERSIONS

(These conversions are rounded for convenience)

Ingredient	Cups/Tablespoons/ Teaspoons	Ounces	Grams/Milliliters
Butter	1 cup/ 16 tablespoons/ 2 sticks	8 ounces	230 grams
Cheese, shredded	1 cup	4 ounces	110 grams
Cream cheese	1 tablespoon	0.5 ounce	14.5 grams
Cornstarch	1 tablespoon	0.3 ounce	8 grams
Flour, all-purpose	1 cup/1 tablespoon	4.5 ounces/0.3 ounce	125 grams/8 grams
Flour, whole wheat	1 cup	4 ounces	120 grams
Fruit, dried	1 cup	4 ounces	120 grams
Fruits or veggies, chopped	1 cup	5 to 7 ounces	145 to 200 grams
Fruits or veggies, puréed	1 cup	8.5 ounces	245 grams
Honey, maple syrup, or corn syrup	1 tablespoon	0.75 ounce	20 grams
Liquids: cream, milk, water, or juice	1 cup	8 fluid ounces	240 milliliters
Oats	1 cup	5.5 ounces	150 grams
Salt	1 teaspoon	0.2 ounces	6 grams
Spices: cinnamon, cloves, ginger, or nutmeg (ground)	1 teaspoon	0.2 ounce	5 milliliters
Sugar, brown, firmly packed	1 cup	7 ounces	200 grams
Sugar, white	1 cup/1 tablespoon	7 ounces/0.5 ounce	200 grams/12.5 grams
Vanilla extract	1 teaspoon	0.2 ounce	4 grams

OVEN TEMPERATURES

Fahrenheit	Celsius	Gas Mark
225°	110°	1/4
250°	120°	1/2
275°	140°	1
300°	150°	2
325°	160°	3
350°	180°	4
375°	190°	5
400°	200°	6
425°	220°	7
450°	230°	8

Index

A

agave nectar
    Granola Wedges, 114
Air-Fried Plantains with Avocado-Mango
    Relish, 103
almond meal
    Crusted Pork Medallions with Rubbed
      Sage, 30
almonds
    Granola Wedges, 114
    Sweet and Spicy Almonds, 91
Ancho Sweet Potato Strings, 78
Apple Galette, 138
apples
    Mini Corn Pups, 117
    Spiced Apple Chips, 95
applesauce
    Granola Wedges, 114
    Veggie and Chickpea Nuggets, 118
aquafaba
    "N'awlins" Tofu, 47
    Zucchini Soldiers, 113
Asian Sweet Potato and Shrimp Crisps, 70–71
avocado
    Air-Fried Plantains with Avocado-Mango
      Relish, 103
Avocado Deviled Eggs, 7

B

bacon
    Buffalo Brussels Sprouts, 65
Baja Pork Fajitas, 21
balsamic glaze
    Easy Balsamic-Roasted Vegetables, 58

Banana-Coconut Rolls, 129
bananas
    Grilled Cheese and Grilled PBB
      Sandwiches, 122
BBQ Tempeh Sticks, 121
beans
    black
      Black Bean and Sweet Potato Burgers, 37
      Vegan Taquitos, 109
    cannellini
      Roasted Garlic and Bean Dip, 84
    great Northern
      Roasted Garlic and Bean Dip, 84
    green
      Lemon-Pepper Green Beans, 69
    white
      Roasted Garlic and Bean Dip, 84
beef
    Shish Kebabs, 52
    Zesty Orange Rib-Eye Skewers, 51
beets
    Roasted Beet Hummus, 87
bell pepper
    Air-Fried Plantains with Avocado-Mango
      Relish, 103
    Baja Pork Fajitas, 21
    Easy Balsamic-Roasted Vegetables, 58
    Summer Veggie Kebabs, 42
    Sweet Potato Hash, 74
    Zesty Orange Rib-Eye Skewers, 51
Best-Ever 5-Ingredient Air Fryer Chocolate
    Cake, 134
Black Bean and Sweet Potato Burgers, 37
Blackberry Cheesecake Chimichangas, 130

Blueberry French Toast Muffins, 4
Bragg Liquid Aminos
    Teriyaki Chicken with Broccoli and Carrots, 16
bran cereal
    Herb-Crusted Pork Chops, 26
bread
    Blueberry French Toast Muffins, 4
    Grilled Cheese and Grilled PBB
        Sandwiches, 122
breadcrumbs
    Broccoli Tots, 125
    Roasted Stuffed Tomatoes, 62
    Turkey Koftas, 41
    Veggie and Chickpea Nuggets, 118
    Zucchini Soldiers, 113
broccoli
    Teriyaki Chicken with Broccoli and
        Carrots, 16
    Veggie and Chickpea Nuggets, 118
Broccoli Tots, 125
Brussels sprouts
    Buffalo Brussels Sprouts, 65
    Farro with Shaved Brussels Sprouts, 61
Buffalo Brussels Sprouts, 65

C

cake
    Best-Ever 5-Ingredient Air Fryer Chocolate
        Cake, 134
carrots
    Teriyaki Chicken with Broccoli and Carrots,
        16
    Veggie and Chickpea Nuggets, 118
cauliflower rice
    Jerk Tempeh with Toasted Coconut Cauli
        Rice, 34
cereal
    bran
        Herb-Crusted Pork Chops, 26
    whole-grain
        "N'awlins" Tofu, 47

cheese
    blue
        Buffalo Brussels Sprouts, 65
    cheddar
        Broccoli Tots, 125
        Vegan Taquitos, 109
    goat
        Farro with Shaved Brussels Sprouts, 61
        Flatbread Veggie Pizzas, 25
    Grilled Cheese and Grilled PBB
        Sandwiches, 122
    Gruyère
        Veggie Frittata, 8
    mozzarella
        Italian Quesadillas, 110
    Parmesan
        Easy Balsamic-Roasted Vegetables, 58
        Eggplant Bruschetta with Roasted
            Polenta, 66
        Florentine Breakfast Casserole, 3
        Garlic-Parmesan Chickpeas, 83
        Polenta Fries, 96
        Roasted Stuffed Tomatoes, 62
        Salmon with Kale and Mushrooms in
            Truffle Oil, 18–19
        Stuffed Cremini Mushrooms, 57
    vegan
        Garlic-Parmesan Chickpeas, 83
chicken
    Moroccan Chicken Skewers, 48
    Teriyaki Chicken with Broccoli and
        Carrots, 16
chickpeas
    Falafel Kebabs, 38
    Garlic-Parmesan Chickpeas, 83
    Roasted Beet Hummus, 87
    Veggie and Chickpea Nuggets, 118
Chili-Lime Taro Chips, 100
chimichangas
    Blackberry Cheesecake Chimichangas, 130
chocolate chips

Best-Ever 5-Ingredient Air Fryer Chocolate
　　Cake, 134
cilantro
　　Avocado Deviled Eggs, 7
coconut
　　Banana-Coconut Rolls, 129
　　Jerk Tempeh with Toasted Coconut Cauli
　　　Rice, 34
coconut milk
　　Banana-Coconut Rolls, 129
coleslaw mix
　　Vegetable Spring Rolls, 22
cookies
　　Gingered Almond Cookies, 141
cornbread mix
　　Mini Corn Pups, 117
cream cheese
　　Blackberry Cheesecake Chimichangas, 130
Crispy Cajun Sweet Potato Wedges, 73
Crusted Pork Medallions with Rubbed Sage, 30
Curried Sweet Potato Fritters, 77

E

Easy Balsamic-Roasted Vegetables, 58
eggplant
　　Summer Veggie Kebabs, 42
Eggplant Bruschetta with Roasted Polenta, 66
eggs
　　Avocado Deviled Eggs, 7
　　Blueberry French Toast Muffins, 4
　　Curried Sweet Potato Fritters, 77
　　Florentine Breakfast Casserole, 3
　　"Hard Boiled" Air Fry Egg, 6
　　Traditional Deviled Eggs, 7
　　Veggie Frittata, 8
Everything Pita Chips, 88

F

Falafel Kebabs, 38
Farro with Shaved Brussels Sprouts, 61
Flatbread Veggie Pizzas, 25

Florentine Breakfast Casserole, 3
frankfurters
　　Mini Corn Pups, 117

G

garam masala
　　Parsnip Chips with Garam Masala, 92
Garlic-Parmesan Chickpeas, 83
ginger
　　Gingered Almond Cookies, 141
Gingered Almond Cookies, 141
Granola Wedges, 114
green beans
　　Lemon-Pepper Green Beans, 69
Grilled Cheese and Grilled PBB Sandwiches, 122

H

"Hard Boiled" Air Fry Egg, 6
　　Avocado Deviled Eggs, 7
　　Traditional Deviled Eggs, 7
hash browns
　　Florentine Breakfast Casserole, 3
Herb-Crusted Pork Chops, 26
honey
　　Granola Wedges, 114
hot dogs
　　Mini Corn Pups, 117
hummus
　　Roasted Beet Hummus, 87

I

Italian Quesadillas, 110

J

Jerk Tempeh with Toasted Coconut Cauli Rice, 34

K

kale
　　Salmon with Kale and Mushrooms in Truffle
　　　Oil, 18–19
kumquats
　　Pear-Kumquat Tart, 133

L

Lemon-Pepper Green Beans, 69

M

mango
   Air-Fried Plantains with Avocado-Mango
      Relish, 103
mayonnaise
   Avocado Deviled Eggs, 7
   Traditional Deviled Eggs, 7
Mini Corn Pups, 117
Montego Bay Turnip Chips, 104
Moroccan Chicken Skewers, 48
mushrooms
   Italian Quesadillas, 110
   Portabella Fajitas, 15
   Salmon with Kale and Mushrooms in Truffle
      Oil, 18–19
   Stuffed Cremini Mushrooms, 57
   Vegetable Spring Rolls, 22
   Veggie Frittata, 8
mustard
   Herb-Crusted Pork Chops, 26
   Traditional Deviled Eggs, 7

N

"N'awlins" Tofu, 47
Neufchâtel
   Blackberry Cheesecake Chimichangas, 130

O

oats
   Granola Wedges, 114
   Strawberry Crisp, 137

P

parsley
   Falafel Kebabs, 38
   Turkey Koftas, 41
Parsnip Chips with Garam Masala, 92
peanut butter
   Grilled Cheese and Grilled PBB Sandwiches, 122

Pear-Kumquat Tart, 133
peas
   Curried Sweet Potato Fritters, 77
   Simple Salmon with Pea Puree, 29
Pistachio-Crusted Shrimp with Asian Dipping
   Sauce, 44–45
pitas
   Everything Pita Chips, 88
pizza
   Flatbread Veggie Pizzas, 25
plantains
   Air-Fried Plantains with Avocado-Mango
      Relish, 103
polenta
   Eggplant Bruschetta with Roasted
      Polenta, 66
Polenta Fries, 96
pork chops
   Herb-Crusted Pork Chops, 26
pork medallions
   Crusted Pork Medallions with Rubbed
      Sage, 30
pork ribs
   Baja Pork Fajitas, 21
Portabella Fajitas, 15
potatoes
   Ancho Sweet Potato Strings, 78
   Asian Sweet Potato and Shrimp Crisps, 70–71
   Black Bean and Sweet Potato Burgers, 37
   Crispy Cajun Sweet Potato Wedges, 73
   Curried Sweet Potato Fritters, 77
   Florentine Breakfast Casserole, 3
   Sweet Potato Hash, 74
   Sweet Potato Toasts, 11

Q

quesadillas
   Italian Quesadillas, 110

R

relish
   Traditional Deviled Eggs, 7

rice
   brown
      Black Bean and Sweet Potato Burgers, 37
      Vegan Taquitos, 109
   cauliflower
      Jerk Tempeh with Toasted Coconut Cauli
         Rice, 34
Roasted Beet Hummus, 87
Roasted Garlic and Bean Dip, 84
Roasted Stuffed Tomatoes, 62
rutabaga
   Chipotle Rutabaga Chips, 99

S

salmon
   Simple Salmon with Pea Puree, 29
Salmon with Kale and Mushrooms in Truffle
   Oil, 18–19
Shish Kebabs, 52
shrimp
   Asian Sweet Potato and Shrimp Crisps, 70–71
   Pistachio-Crusted Shrimp with Asian
      Dipping Sauce, 44–45
   Sriracha Shrimp, 33
Simple Salmon with Pea Puree, 29
soy sauce
   Teriyaki Chicken with Broccoli and
      Carrots, 16
Spiced Apple Chips, 95
spinach
   Florentine Breakfast Casserole, 3
   Italian Quesadillas, 110
   Veggie Frittata, 8
squash
   Flatbread Veggie Pizzas, 25
   Italian Quesadillas, 110
Sriracha Shrimp, 33
steak
   Shish Kebabs, 52
   Zesty Orange Rib-Eye Skewers, 51
Strawberry Crisp, 137

Stuffed Cremini Mushrooms, 57
Summer Veggie Kebabs, 42
Sweet and Spicy Almonds, 91
sweet potato
   Ancho Sweet Potato Strings, 78
   Asian Sweet Potato and Shrimp Crisps,
      70–71
   Black Bean and Sweet Potato Burgers, 37
   Crispy Cajun Sweet Potato Wedges, 73
   Curried Sweet Potato Fritters, 77
Sweet Potato Hash, 74
Sweet Potato Toasts, 11

T

tahini
   Roasted Beet Hummus, 87
taquitos
   Vegan Taquitos, 109
taro root
   Chili-Lime Taro Chips, 100
tater tots
   Florentine Breakfast Casserole, 3
tempeh
   BBQ Tempeh Sticks, 121
   Jerk Tempeh with Toasted Coconut Cauli
      Rice, 34
Teriyaki Chicken with Broccoli and Carrots, 16
tofu
   "N'awlins" Tofu, 47
tomatoes
   Avocado Deviled Eggs, 7
   Baja Pork Fajitas, 21
   Flatbread Veggie Pizzas, 25
   Roasted Stuffed Tomatoes, 62
   Shish Kebabs, 52
   Summer Veggie Kebabs, 42
   Veggie Frittata, 8
tortillas
   Apple Galette, 138
   Blackberry Cheesecake Chimichangas, 130
   Flatbread Veggie Pizzas, 25

Italian Quesadillas, 110
Pear-Kumquat Tart, 133
Vegan Taquitos, 109
Traditional Deviled Eggs, 7
Turkey Koftas, 41
turnips
Montego Bay Turnip Chips, 104

V

Vegan Taquitos, 109
Vegetable Spring Rolls, 22
Veggie and Chickpea Nuggets, 118
Veggie Frittata, 8

Y

yogurt
Moroccan Chicken Skewers, 48

Z

Zesty Orange Rib-Eye Skewers, 51
zucchini
Roasted Stuffed Tomatoes, 62
Stuffed Cremini Mushrooms, 57
Summer Veggie Kebabs, 42
Zucchini Soldiers, 113

About the Authors and Photographer

Bonnie Matthews is a food photographer, cookbook author, and illustrator. She lives in Costa Mesa, California with her two rescue cats, Otis and Mergle. When Bonnie is not creating recipes or photographing food, she's drawing and painting for children's books and magazines. She's illustrated 25 books for children, including the award-winning "What To Do" series. In her spare time, she escapes to tiny islands and snorkels to get inspiration for the characters she draws. She is also the author of *The Freekeh Cookbook*, *Hot & Hip Grilling Secrets*, *Hot & Hip Healthy Gluten-Free Cooking*, and *The Eat Your Way Healthy at Trader Joe's Cookbook*.

Dawn E. Hall is co-owner of The J&D Food Company and co-creator of Them Balls, a fusion meatball brand. Dawn lives in Orange County, California with her husband, Jonathan, and their twin sons, Solomon and Jameson. Besides catering where she specializes in menu and recipe building, Dawn loves creating new meatball ideas in the test kitchen. In her spare time, Dawn enjoys power naps, taking train rides with her family in search of good eats and excursions off the beaten path.

Also by Bonnie Matthews

Notes

Notes

Notes

Notes

Notes